CONTEMPLATIVE DRUIDRY:
PEOPLE PRACTICE AND POTENTIAL

JAMES NICHOL

Foreword by Philip Carr-Gomm

Deep Peace of the Quiet Earth: the Nature Mysticism of Druidry

CONTEMPLATIVE DRUIDRY

Copyright © 2014 James Nichol

All rights reserved

ISBN-10: 1500807206

ISBN-13: 978-1500807207

Acknowledgements

First of all I offer my thanks to the 14 people who participated in this project with me by responding to a series of questions (see Appendix 1). They are, in alphabetical order of first names: David Popely, Elaine Knight, Eve Adams, JJ Middleway, Joanna Vander Hoeven, Julie Bond, Karen Webb, Katy Jordan, Mark Rosher, Nimue Brown, Penny Billington, Robert Kyle, Rosa Davis and Tom Brown. Their contributions, some made in face-to-face interviews and others as written responses to the questions, are the heart of the book. Extensive extracts from their responses are presented in the 10 numbered chapters. Brief biographical information about the contributors themselves can be found at Appendix 8.

I thank another 16 people for agreeing to re-publish their comments in two threads from the Contemplative Druidry Facebook group. They are: Alix Sandra Huntley-Speirs, Andrew Jones, Ani Ashford, Emma Restall Orr, Beer Schipper, Cat Treadwell, Chris Brolls, Criss Glover, Dawn N Jodie Diaz-Ruiz, Bishop Mark Pius Charlton, Nico Vermaas, Pascale Titley, Reg Amor, Stewart Moonhare Talmage, Thomas Harris and William Brochfael Rathouse. The threads, on contemplation and mysticism and on pilgrimage, appear as Appendices 6 and 7.

I thank Philip Carr-Gomm, Chosen Chief of the Order of Bards, Ovates and Druids for his early support on this project as well as for his foreword to this book, *Deep Peace of the Quiet Earth, the Nature Mysticism of Druidry*. Thanks too to Michael Houseman, Directeur d'Etudes at the Ecole Pratique des Hautes Etudes, Paris, for being a critically supportive reader of the text as it developed.

I owe five of the above-mentioned people a second round of thanks: Julie Bond and Robert Kyle for offering the practices in Appendices 3 and 5; Nimue Brown for her support in proof-reading and the processes of publication and publicity; Rosa Davis for five years of Druid contemplative conversations, seamlessly interwoven with our OBOD mentoring conversations; and Elaine Knight for sharing her life with me, discussing the project as it developed, and offering invaluable feedback and support.

Finally I thank teachers and practice frameworks from traditions that have influenced me. I am particularly grateful for the experience of the OBOD distance learning course, to which I owe my Druid centre of gravity, and I include my students as well as my mentors, and also everyone involved in the design, co-ordination and administration of this course. I likewise thank everyone who has played a part in the Druid contemplative group in Gloucestershire since its beginning in July 2012. Outside the ranks of Druidry, I wish to acknowledge the influence of the London Transpersonal Centre, Shambhala Buddhism and the published work of R.J. Stewart and Sally Kempton. All have provided working methods that I continue to draw from, indirectly inspiring this book.

Table of contents

Acknowledgements   3

Table of contents   5

Foreword by Philip Carr-Gomm   7

Introduction   14

Part 1   **People - Introduction**   25

Chapter 1   Childhood Openings   27

Chapter 2   Images, Ideas and Influences   35

Chapter 3   Questing and Discovery   50

Chapter 4   Druid Identity and Values   59

Part 2   **Practice – Introduction**   70

Chapter 5   Formal Sitting Meditations   72

Chapter 6   Being in Nature, Walking the Land   85

Chapter 7   Group Practice, Life Practice   93

Chapter 8   Awen   101

Part 3	Potential – Introduction	113
Chapter 9	What Practice Can Do	115
Chapter 10	Benefits for the Community	125

Reflections and Conclusions 134

Appendices

Appendix 1	Interview Questions	147
Appendix 2	Contemplative Day Programme	149
Appendix 3	Twelve Holy Nights Retreat	150
Appendix 4	Morning Practice Framework	157
Appendix 5	Aspiration Prayer to Taliesin	161
Appendix 6	Contemplation and Mysticism	166
Appendix 7	Pilgrimage	177
Appendix 8	Contributors' Brief Biographies	188

Deep Peace of the Quiet Earth: the Nature Mysticism of Druidry

Foreword by Philip Carr-Gomm

Nothing is stronger than an idea whose time has come.

Victor Hugo

We all know that Druidry is a magical path – Druids wear robes and conduct rituals with wands and candles, invocations to the directions, prayers to the gods. In a world sorely lacking in meaningful ritual, it can feel like a balm to the soul to engage in actions that are not obviously utilitarian, that are designed to help us into a deeper engagement in life – to give expression to our belief in a world of Spirit that infuses this physical world with energies that bring healing and inspiration. And yet it can sometimes feel as if modern Druidry's concern with ritual has placed too great an emphasis on the magical, at the expense of its equally important mystical concerns.

An interest in mysticism, and in the use of contemplation, meditation and devotional practices that foster the aims of the mystic, has always been present in the modern Druid movement, but in the excitement of Druidry's renaissance over the last twenty or so years, it is probably fair to say that the balance of attention has tipped towards the magical in Druidry, and that now it is time we paid more attention to the mystical. This book, therefore, is published at just the right moment in the unfolding story of Druidry as a vibrant contemporary spirituality, and gives voice to "an idea whose time has come".

The magic of Druidry is based upon the knowledge that our actions, thoughts and feelings can influence the world for good, and can be enhanced in their effectiveness through the use of magical techniques. The mysticism in Druidry is based upon the experience of changes in consciousness: feelings of Oneness, of union with Spirit, God or Goddess, and the world of Nature, and it is perhaps best qualified as 'Nature Mysticism' or 'Natural Mysticism', to distinguish it from approaches that emphasise only union with Deity, or even a separation from the physical world in the pursuit of the Divine. One of the beauties of Druidry is that it is not a dogmatic or formulaic approach – no 'one size fits all', and those of us who follow the Druid way are encouraged to craft our own practice in accordance with our inner guidance, our needs and wishes. And so, one person may feel more drawn to the magical, another to the mystical, but I'd imagine most of us need a mixture of both approaches, just as we need a range of practices to bring a sense of wholeness to our personal and spiritual lives. The philosopher Ken Wilber writes that we leave out any one of these practices at our peril: meditation, psychological – particularly interpersonal – work, some form of 'sacred' movement or exercise, and a study of spiritual teachings. To that list we might add some form of devotional practice and frequent drinking at the well of Bardism – the world of myth, story, poetry and song. Each of these practices informs the other, so that the world of the Bard can inspire us towards meditation, for example, while meditation can enable us to appreciate more deeply the offerings of the Bard. Sacred movement, such as Qi Gong or Yoga, can be a meditation in itself, and ensures we ground our awareness in our bodies, while meditation without psychological inquiry, as Wilber stresses, can provoke imbalances which negate its value.

The OBOD course in Druidry attempts to incorporate psychological work with teachings on meditation and an encouragement of the Bardic arts, but although there are some movement exercises suggested, a distance learning programme cannot effectively teach a system of psycho-spiritual physical exercise. Yoga, Tai Chi, Qi Gong, have all been developed over centuries to fulfil our need for such an activity, and perhaps one day specifically Druidic systems will be developed. One such system, known as Wyda, that claims to derive from Druidry, has already been promoted in a book only available in German, published in 1993. Mgr. Mael, the founder of the Celtic Orthodox Church in Brittany, who was a Druid and a friend of the founder of OBOD, Nuinn, received a series of meditative physical exercises in a vision, and taught these as a system of 'Celtic Yoga'. Philip Shallcrass has developed a series of exercises based on the Ogham that he teaches in the British Druid Order's Ovate course, and a few years ago I was given a simple movement meditation exercise after asking in spirit for many years for a meditation we as Druids could share widely. You can find it on www.druidry.org. (Search for 'Deep Peace of the Tree Meditation'.)

All of these attempts to create a specifically Druid method of sacred movement raise the issues of validity and authenticity, which apply equally to any attempts to offer methods of Druid meditation. Are such attempts valid, when so many other highly developed systems already exist? And are they not 'fake', having been so recently invented, while the Eastern systems are clearly genuine having been around for centuries? As regards validity, a method that is valid is one that works, however young or old it is. As regards inauthenticity, if a method is pretending to be one thing, while in reality being another, then that is indeed inauthentic. If Mgr. Mael had pretended his system of Celtic Yoga was practised by the ancient Druids, this would have been inauthentic. But since he clearly stated he had received the exercises in a series of dreams, his system is authentically what he stated it to be: a method received in an altered state of consciousness. A false claim to ancient lineage made for a system that has only been recently created renders it inauthentic, but if no such claim is made, can we use the term 'Druid' to describe it?

Contemporary Druidry is a flourishing creative spirituality that is inspiring people the world over. Is it a closed system that was only open to new inputs several thousand years ago? Or is it an open system that allows for development and evolution? Modern Druidry has been growing and evolving for the last three hundred years and if we were to throw out any additions to its body of teachings and ritual practice made during this time, we would be left with a small and unworkable set of conjectures. If we didn't allow ourselves to call something Druidic that has only recently been created, we would have no Druidry to practice. But this shouldn't mean we can call simply anything Druidic. Druidry has specific features which help to define what it has become and how it is evolving. In particular, Druidry has developed into a spiritual and philosophical approach that embraces embodiment that does not deny the gifts of the physical world and the body. In addition it cultivates both inwardness and outwardness – an appreciation of the inner and outer worlds that fosters an engagement with the Earth and with community as much as it encourages an exploration of the depths of the soul and merging with the Divine. The evidence of the centrality of this approach can be found in Druidry's love of Nature, its reverence for the Earth, and its cornerstone ritual observance: the Eightfold Wheel of the Year. These characteristics define Druidry and they also tell us what it is not.

And so when it comes to the subject of this book, contemplation and meditation within Druidry, it seems perfectly reasonable to me to talk in terms of 'Druid meditation' or to describe techniques or approaches as Druidic, if they fall within the ethos of Druidry, because that ethos is specific: it does not attempt to subjugate, transcend or deny the body. There is no emphasis on the illusory nature of the physical world. The goal in Druidry, and hence in meditation for Druids, is to enhance our engagement with our embodied life, not to distance or separate ourselves from it.

Humans have been borrowing from each other since the first person used another's flint or axe. Scratch the surface of any religion and you find it is made up of a number of influences and elements. Examine a ritual text or liturgy and you can see the bricolage at work. We naturally understand the common sense in not re-inventing the wheel, even though we might adapt or embellish the wheel we make for ourselves. And so when looking at the question of meditation, I don't believe we need to concern ourselves, beyond an honouring of whatever facts can be determined, with the source of our meditation techniques and styles. Mindfulness, the focusing of awareness on the breath, the scanning of our body awareness as practised in vipassana, for example, may all be sourced in Buddhism, but Hindu and Jain scholars will say that such practices were already in use before the arrival of the Buddha, and if any of the theories of our common Indo-Aryan ancestry turns out to be true, and the ancient Druids drew their teachings from the same well as the Brahmins or Jains, then in using these techniques we are indeed drawing from the same source of our tradition as Druids. Whether or not this is historically the case, the reality is that there is nothing more natural than scanning our body with our awareness, sensing our breath, letting go of outside distractions to settle our restless minds and hearts, to come to a sense of stillness. And if we do find ourselves using techniques that seem to have originated elsewhere, we can embrace them in that same warm spirit of inclusion shown by the Benedictine monk Bede Griffiths who lived in Bangalore as a 'Christian Yogi', and became known as Swami Dayananda ('Bliss of Compassion').

This spirit of inclusion, of Universalism that happily recognises the gifts that come from many different sources, can be found right here in the pages of this book. Here we find that mystical experience is not confined to the few 'adepts' or 'evolved souls' who stand out from the masses (an image fostered in both Eastern and Western spiritual literature) but that a democratisation exists, or has perhaps occurred in modern times. All the contributors have had access to altered states of consciousness, unforgettable moments of bliss or insight that suggests the mystical state is a natural one within everyone's reach. And so it is fitting that the book reflects this empowerment and this movement away from the individual teacher who is marked out from his or her contemporaries. Instead of one voice, we hear many, and the book itself reflects the movement from individual to community, from 'me' to 'we' in the collective, in which we discover our common voice of humanity and at the same time our uniqueness.

The book ends with suggestions for the future, for ways in which the contemplative approach can become more prominent within contemporary Druidry and OBOD. With its publication, and with its message being heard by others, I have a strong feeling that the hopes expressed by James and his fellow contributors will soon be realised!

Philip Carr-Gomm, 24 September 2014

Introduction

Why I am writing this book

On 22 June 2007 my centre of gravity shifted. It was late morning. I was just outside the Scottish Border town of Melrose, drawn in three possible directions. One was up the hills at the back of the town – the Eildon Hills, the hollow hills where the Queen of Efland took Thomas the Rhymer; True Thomas as he became. The second was the fine, if half-ruined, Abbey and its grounds; a place of Green Man carvings, fruit trees, and the heart of Robert the Bruce. The third was the banks of the Tweed.

I took the third option and walked into a wholly unexpected and not at all dramatic epiphany. It was triggered simply by noticing and contemplating a wild rose, growing on the banks of the river. It lasted a few moments, just long enough for me to register it, and to experience a subtle shift of awareness in consequence. For some weeks I woke up every day with a sense of joy and connection. Months later, I wrote the verse that expressed it:

> I am Rose. I am wild Rose.
>
> I am Rose at Midsummer.
>
> The river flows by me.
>
> Fragile, I shiver in the wind.
>
> And I am the heart's core, mover of mountains.

From that time on – gradually rather than suddenly – I've been tilted towards practices that support a fuller presence within the stream of passing experience. For me, 'contemplation' in its richest sense enables a transfigured here-and-now, and the dissolving of subject/object distinctions within it. The value of contemplation is in being alert to that possibility, indeed celebratory of that possibility and its transformative potential. Contemplation can have many benefits – aesthetic, cognitive, ethical, therapeutic. Contemplative practice is an effective technology of self. Yet it always points beyond self, as commonly understood. I link it to a view of grace.

I imagine that contemplative experience is at least as old as humanity as we know it. It is certainly visible for as far back as we have the evidence to see. I'm thinking specifically of the sacred observation and connectedness that clearly went into Palaeolithic cave art and carving (1). By the time of early metal working cultures, we find words for contemplation in senses that link observation to deep insight, or to the realm of the numinous, in a number of Indo-European languages. Old Irish 'dercad' literally means 'looking', with connotations of deep understanding and fixing the mind upon something in meditation. In Sanskrit, 'darsana' may be translated as either 'seeing' or 'philosophy' – which always has a connotation of sacred knowledge (2). Greek 'theoria' is a vision of the divine (3). The Latin word 'templum' is the source for English contemplation. Originally a 'templum' was ground marked out from which to interpret the flight of birds. The activity itself was 'contemplatio' (4).

Anchoring the experience

For some time after Melrose I was uncertain about how to anchor my new experience; a ridiculous uncertainty since such an experience cannot be anchored. But the desire was there, in a more generous view not to be mocked if it could lead to favourable changes in my life and practice. I wondered what changes I might need to make. I had a long familiarity with 'inner' working, from three sources. The first was a training in 'active imagination' from the Jungian influenced London Transpersonal Centre, at that time run by Ian Gordon-Brown and Barbara Summers. The second was a discipline of contemplative pathworking largely based on R. J. Stewart's work. The third was sacred grove and light body meditation taught by the Order of Bards, Ovates and Druids (OBOD), which develops and deepens throughout the Order's distance learning courses.

It seemed that the Melrose experience asked for something different, more direct. I had learned a Buddhist style of sitting meditation many years before with Shambhala, a Tibetan Vajrayana school, which I revisited from time to time. Would this be my direction? For a time I thought so. Late in 2010 I gave an interview to a local radio station in which I talked about it – an edited version is on the OBOD website in the section on Druidry and Dharmic religions. I also read Jason Kirkey's book *The Salmon in the Spring: the Ecology of Celtic Spirituality* (5) which shows how we can be inspired and resourced by a second spiritual path, whilst fully integrating it within an expanded vision of the first.

Kirkey had entered a tradition of Irish Earth-based spirituality and Shamanism following a realisation that "nature does not require our belief. It is right there for us to experience". Later he found that an over-identified 'attachment' to his own tradition became narrow and constraining. He addressed this through sitting meditation and study at the Shambala inspired Naropa University in Colorado. He then integrated the new learning into his original tradition. He saw this personal journey as a thread within a larger, collective story; one in which spiritual traditions are moving through a process of re-imagination, and of integration into the new story of the 21st century.

In 2011 I refreshed my own experience of Shambhala and also spent time with other Buddhist groups. At the end of that time I decided to launch a 'contemplative exploration' for myself and others within Druidry, starting with OBOD, where I have a role in mentoring Bards and Ovates engaged in the Order's distance learning programme. In October 2011, I wrote about my exploration idea to Philip Carr-Gomm, the Chief of OBOD, receiving encouraging feedback about what I then called 'the ghost of a seed' of a project. I formally committed myself to the project through a ritual of dedication to the Goddess in her Wisdom aspect at Samhuinn of that year.

Despite my own practice choices at that time, I chose the term 'contemplative' to provide a more open frame for the exploration than a term like 'shamatha vipashyana meditation', or the more generic 'mindfulness meditation'. Indeed part of my interest in developing this work was that I recognised my older practices as contemplative too. They had worked well for a long period.

Joining with Others

I turned outwards to my community, asking what contemplative spirituality means to modern Druids. My priority was to find out how other Druids experience and make sense of contemplative practice. In April 2012 I wrote an article, *Contemplative Practice*, for the OBOD magazine Touchstone and, as a starting point, deliberately chose a broadly based definition of how contemplative spirituality is understood in today's pluralistic and questing world. This is one used in 2012 by the Contemplative Studies Initiative at Brown University, Providence, Rhode Island (www.brown.edu/academics/contemplative-studies) who said, "while various methods to attain contemplative states of consciousness can be found in such religious practices as chanting, prayer, ritual performance, and meditation, such states can also be found in a wide variety of non-religious practices such as music, dance, drama, writing poetry or prose, painting, sculpting, and even the intent observation of the natural world."

I did wonder about the separation between "religious" and "non-religious" practices ('religious' being such a tricky word). And – as a Druid, with the Melrose experience behind me - I noticed myself being a bit reactive about the use of the word "even" before "intent observation of the natural world". But I was generally happy to stand behind this inclusive and enabling definition.

The *Touchstone* article invited correspondence, received correspondence, and began a process of connecting with people. This led on to a contemplative exploration day in Stroud on 7 July 2012. Six of us used the time to listen to and reflect on our stories, feelings and thoughts about contemplative practice within Druidry and what it means to us. Many of us were involved in a solo practice, but more than one described how hard this can be to maintain without shared opportunities to slow down, to enter a Nemeton of interwoven silence and reflection, and deepen practice together.

When people later shared their reflections about this day for another article, one participant said that she had experienced "far more" than the anticipated "gentle day" and felt "opened, stirred, deepened and confirmed ... in my own spiritual practice" after recognising the common threads that had brought us together. "I was left with a deep sense of your continuing companionship along my solitary way". Another pointed out how "lean ritual and a simple slow process created a spaciousness which allowed a deepening of my own experience". She also talked about the way in which she had heard group members "speaking from the heart".

Overall, people articulated a sense that a particular stillness-allowing simplicity of structure enables a certain kind of presence, and that this can be a powerful experience. It was described in terms like authenticity and flow – silence, yet also laughter and wildness; a trusting of process and allowing for "not knowing: always such a rich resource for nurturing and learning". The day had an affirming and renewing quality and we agreed that we would continue meeting and developing this approach to our Druid practice further. One member summed the experience up in these lines:

> Six Druids sit silent
>
> Speak, seek, remember, laugh:
>
> Gentle healing day.

I felt that the idea of group working was fully vindicated. The group stayed in contact and others joined our list. Some came via the Contemplative Druidry Facebook group, which I launched in August 2012 with the support of three other administrators drawn with links to three Druid groups – OBOD, the Druid Network and the OSN (Order of the Sacred Nemeton, a monastic Druid Order). Two of the Facebook group's threads are republished in this book with the permission of the posters and commenters, adding an international dimension to an exploration otherwise based in England and to a large extent in a single English county. The Gloucestershire group itself, slowly growing larger and itself now extending beyond OBOD, gathered again for two more days in 2013, and in October of that year we decided on an annual cycle of monthly meetings, with full days in May and November and shorter meetings in the other months.

Within a relatively short period of time this group had co-created a distinctive contemplative culture, and it is possible to point to key moments in its emergence. Thus on the 13 March 2013 day, JJ Middleway spoke of a connection based on "like intent" rather than "like-mindedness". It felt to me that this intent had grown out of the still simplicity of the shared space we created as our time together developed. Our practices are structurally simple and provide for a spacious opening up of possibilities: minimal facilitator input, lean ritual, hardly any formal devotional activity and no scripts (except at times when singing or chanting). We are happy to sit in silent meditation together on the basis of diverse inward practices, holding the individual path in the collective embrace of the group.

On the 19 October 2013 day, we deepened our collective sense of Awen, which we have increasingly understood as a field where we are touched and inspired to enter a more open and receptive quality of relationship within ourselves, within the space and with each other. Nimue Brown, who led us in to our Awen awareness, began by saying: "Awen doesn't have to be invoked. It's always there". Both of these insights, along with our very simplicity of structure, have become part of the group's collective note.

This Gloucestershire group has now settled into a rhythm of meeting every month – with a two hour meeting in most months and a full day in May and November, when we spend more time outside. Whilst it continues to grow and develop, with different inputs, the basic structures remain very simple.

The Book

The idea for this book came out of the contemplative exploration process. Although the book was my idea and I am the author overall, it is a collaborative venture. The chapters which follow are based on a set of questions (see Appendix 1) answered by 15 Druids, including me, either in face-to-face interviews or in writing, between 1 March and 31 July 2014. All are currently resident in England, and practising their Druidry in a largely English context. All are involved in some form of contemplative practice. There is a bias towards the Gloucestershire group – 11 of the 15 contributors are in it. But four are not. I wanted to make it clear that there are other voices in contemplative Druidry. My intention is to offer a polyphonic text, in which interviewees are able to speak directly to the reader, too well represented to suffer from bias in my selection process and too strong and autonomous to be submerged under my narrative framing.

My work within the 10 named chapters can be likened to stringing pearls, with my authorial text (in italics) as the string and interview extracts as the pearls. Readers may note different styles in the responses of the contributors, beyond simple personal differences in approach. This is due to the difference between the oral communication of one-to-one interviewees and the written language of the other contributors.

The 10 chapters which follow are arranged in three parts: people, practice and potential.

The four chapters in part 1 – 'People' – are titled: childhood openings; images, ideas and influences; questing and discovery; Druid identity and values.

The four chapters in part 2 - 'Practice' – are titled: formal solo meditations; being in nature, walking the land; group practice, life practice; Awen.

The two chapters in part 3 - 'Potential' – are titled: what practice can do; benefits for the community.

I end the book with some reflections and conclusions. This is in four sections: what we learn from the chapters; teaching and learning Druid contemplation; Awen; where I stand now.

There are eight appendices. The first is the schedule of questions for interviews. The second is a typical programme for a full day meeting of the Gloucestershire contemplative group. The next three are specific practice offerings by contributors.

Appendices 6 and 7 are threads from the early days (August 2012) of the Contemplative Druidry Facebook group – one on contemplation and mysticism and one on pilgrimage. They are published here with the permission of the posters and commenters. The final appendix provides brief biographical details of the contributors.

I hope this book can do something to raise awareness of the contemplative possibilities, both actualised and still latent, within modern Druidry. It offers a snapshot of people who are currently practising, provides an account of the forms which their practice takes, and suggests potentials for development. And in the wider scheme of things, it is only a beginning.

References

1: Sentier, Elen (2013) *Elen of the ways: following the deer trods: the ancient Shamanism of Britain* Winchester: Moon Books (Shaman Pathways series)

2: *Siva Sutras: the yoga of supreme identity* (1979) Delhi, India: Motilal Banarsidass. (English translation with introduction, commentaries and glossary by Jaideva Singh.)

3: http://en.wikipedia.org.wiki theoria (June 2014)

4: http://en.wikipedia.org.wiki contemplation (June 2014)

5: Kirkey, Jason (2009) *The salmon in the spring: the ecology of Celtic spirituality* San Francisco, CA: Hiraeth Press

Part 1: People

Introduction

Most of this book is based on responses to a series of questions, which I put to the people who agreed to contribute. Some answered in face-to-face interviews, others in writing. These responses give expression and form to the contemplative Druidry of the title, varied in style in ways that reflect their different perspectives and also according to which of the two methods they chose.

I didn't begin with questions about contemplation or contemplative practice. I wanted to get to know my fellow explorers a little better, and to know something of what stands behind their current identification as Druids and their ways of practising Druidry. So the four chapters of this first part are about the contributors as people, about their spiritual journeys and in particular their relationship with Druidry as a specific path.

I asked about early memories of what they might now call spiritual openness and experience and I was surprised by the consistency of responses and the coherence of the picture that emerged. People characterised themselves as children who loved the outdoors, but also had rich interior landscapes fed in many cases by myth and fantasy available through literature and other media. For some, there were openings to liminal spaces, to dimensions not generally discussed or accepted in the wider world. Some asked big questions about the cosmos, about source and meaning –

and were not satisfied by the conventional answers provided. As they grew up, this dissatisfaction manifested in a certain restlessness and questing, and a willingness to experiment with matters of belief, practice and identity in the service of a greater integrity and wholeness. Eventually this would lead to some kind of holding space, or participation in a more or less congenial subculture. In this group, Druidry has been the principal eventual destination for many (not all). Equally, for many of us, it has not been the first or only one. For many the path to Druidry has been a long and winding one. Yet the resulting affiliation is strong, with a powerfully articulated sense of Druid identity and values.

Drawing on the words of the contributors, the following four chapters examine this picture in a little more detail.

Chapter 1: Childhood Openings

Nature and Presence

Three contributors – Penny, Eve and Robert - talk about their connectedness with the outdoors, and in particular trees and plants. For these children there's a liminality in close connection with the land and its life, an opening to the numinous. Penny recalls "being very close to nature and feeling a real connectedness" and, with that "a feeling of Otherness – of Other Presence maybe". Eve talks of "paranormal" experiences "that I didn't have any way of understanding or expressing". Robert talks of the land "being alive" and "how it spoke to me with words that whispered through the trees", specifically naming a Presence (the Watcher) "that I could feel moved through the very land beneath me". He also links this connection with goodness and happiness. "We know ourselves through our feelings; the ones that make us happy are the ones that we're drawn to because they nurture something good within us."

Penny: Like many people I remember, as a young child, incidents of being very close to nature and feeling a real connectedness with trees and plants. I wanted to be out in the open and engaging with nature, tracking and lighting fires, and the only experience of that available at that time was being a Girl Guide. So I lived from camp to camp and hike to hike and loved that. An early and very significant memory is of standing under a beech tree in the rain, yet sheltered and kept dry by the branches. There was a feeling of Otherness – of Other Presence; an intimation of a world beyond the five senses. But there were very limited ways to express that feeling of connection; there was no vocabulary for natural spiritual experience.

Eve: I think the core thing is my true essence, how I have experienced and honoured my true essence through my life. It resides strongly in a love of nature. It is where my heart sings and when I feel most inspired and joyful. The history of that obviously started when I was very little, in the garden, being with the flowers and the trees... I just remember sitting under bushes. I remember sitting under shrubs and bushes. Sitting on the Earth and finding treasures in the Earth... I was actually quite a psychic child so I had experiences, paranormal experiences with nature that I didn't have any way of understanding or expressing. So I was a very sensitive child, and very psychic. There was a period of time when I literally left the garden (we moved to a flat on top of a shop with no garden). This severed my relationship with nature during my adolescent years but the gift in that wound was the discovery of nature in poetry and literature.

Robert: When I was a boy I was always lost in nature. I would spend days in the forest, to me it was alive; it spoke to me with words that whispered amongst the trees. I knew of a presence that I could feel moved through the very land beneath me. I called it The Watcher. We know ourselves through our feelings; the ones that make us happy are the ones that we're drawn to because they nurture something good within us. I remember a very happy childhood; nature generated that happiness through the simple things of water, stone, fire and air. I needed nothing other than the elements, a box of matches and a penknife, those were my tools. I was lucky to be brought up in the country and not in an inner city estate, we were poor, but that didn't seem to matter when I could escape to the forest, there I was a king, living with the animals that ran wild and free.

Woods and Wastes

Another two people talk about the outdoors in ways that don't quite indicate the same psychic sensitivity, but where something seems to hover at the edge of the text nonetheless.

Mark celebrates a time of freedom, happy solitude and green landscapes under the benign protection of his grandparents. Nature doesn't have to be pristine to work its magic. Mark talks of "old bombsites, now re-vegetated and semi-wild". He says, unprompted, "I wouldn't say I made connections with the non-apparent world back then" – thereby introducing the idea into the conversation.

In my own piece, I locate strong images, strong feelings and a compelling story in times I spent with my father, being introduced to the Faerie realm in local woods. Mark and I both talk, in very similar ways, about how much we value the memory of these experiences. This may be partly because of what followed. Mark had a change of regime at home, with the appearance of a Pentecostal step-father (described in Chapter 2). My experience was less dramatic. Over time, my father and I dropped our talks with woodland beings. I recall some sadness at this.

Mark: My father had died when I was young, and I was largely brought up by my grandparents, who moved from Ipswich to Bath in order to allow my mother to work. I was free to play in the woodland and what were probably old bombsites, now re-vegetated and semi-wild. I was happy in my own company (still am) and it was a time when I learned to enjoy the green landscape. I wouldn't say I made connections to the non-apparent world back then, but it was a good time and remains a precious memory.

James: When I look for early signs of natural development, a few things come up. They have to do with the impact of strong images working together with strong feelings, and the stories that went with them. When I was 3, 4 and 5 years old I used to go for walks with my father in some woods. They were in easy walking distance from home and we'd walk among the trees. It was a companionable time, a time when I was very close to my father. He would introduce me to the little people who lived in the trees, in hidden houses there, in and around the trees. And we would greet and talk to them. And we would share the magic of the woods and the hidden life that's in them. It was just a brief period in my life and it flashed past very quickly. Yet these special moments of connection lit up my world and the memories have lasted a life time.

Innerworld and Otherworld Experiences

Two other people speak briefly yet suggestively about early inner experiences, without specific reference to the natural world outside. Rather, they focus on the psychic domain and non-ordinary perception. These are understood as having a key role in awakening an early spiritual sense. Elaine talks of a "gateway" opened by childhood lucid dreaming – and the need to close it. Tom talks of a very early awareness of realms beyond consensus reality.

Elaine: I believe that I had a form of spiritual life and practice from early childhood. Before I went to school I was a lucid dreamer and at that time both my waking life and my dreaming life had equal weight. However what I encountered in my lucid dream state began to disturb me so I closed down this gateway. I continued to have an awareness of the "otherworld" throughout my childhood and adolescence and I expressed this in my creative writing and my art.

Tom: I would say I was drawn into a spiritual way from a very, very young age. From as far back as I can remember I've been aware that there's more to the world than meets the eye or than most people discuss.

Divinity in the World

Some people go so far as to link their response to the natural world to a sense of the Divine, though not necessarily in a highly theologised sense. JJ is aware from his earliest memories "as a baby almost" of "whatever... the namelessness of spirit", which he links to being "very close to nature". And he calls his father, an "ardent" atheist, "as much of a Druid as I've ever met... blackbirds used to come and eat of his hand". Here the word "Druid" is not used to name a formal affiliation or set of beliefs and practices, but a simple way of being, a stance in the world, manifesting in an openness to wild creatures that is somehow recognised and accepted by them. In a slightly different way, JJ recognises his Catholic mother as a "good soul" so that he can say of his upbringing overall "spirituality in its broadest sense came to me early on". Rosa describes an "ecstatic experience of oneness" when out walking. She was 17 at time, but had been brought up in a non-religious background and had no conceptual or devotional framework for this. It was not until many years later that she linked this experience, and others that succeeded it, to the language of spirituality. Eve reports a similar experience in her later teens. Karen talks of a "more than..." intuition at a very early age, before she could name or articulate it. Then she has her first unitive experience "triggered by a flower". This time she does have a language for it, naming it as "a mystical experience ... Divine in nature" because by the age of 12 or 13 she is already reading on these subjects.

JJ: OK. Well in that case I was aware from my earliest memories and I mean as a baby almost, as a child... of being closely connected with... whatever... the namelessness of spirit, and very close to nature although I lived in the middle of a city... And always aware that beyond the voice in humans and really aware of... more than character, of spirit, though I didn't have a name for it. I mean it's odd, because my mother was a Catholic, I was brought up as a Catholic; my dad was an atheist, ardent atheist even, so I had both, I had a real contrast... and yet he was as much Druid as I've ever met. Blackbirds used to come and eat off his hand. He loved his garden, he loved the earth. And mum was a really good soul - so that spirituality in its broadest sense came to me very early on and in a funny way.

Rosa: My parents were atheists, so I grew up in a non-religious background. When I was 17, I was walking alone along a hilltop in Dorset at sunset. Suddenly everything seemed vivid and wondrous, bathed in unconditioned love with a sense of ecstatic oneness. After this for many years I could recreate a lesser sense of this ecstasy and love by walking, and often chanting made up songs, alone in nature. In my early 30s I began to practice yoga as a means of exercising my body. I experienced the same peace and oneness I had discovered as a teenager, and knowing that yoga could be a spiritual practice I thought – "so this is spirituality". Up 'til then I had no idea what was meant by the word! I then began to explore different ideas and practices including meditation. That was the beginning.

Eve: I had an experience, a particularly formative experience when I was about 18, 17 or 18, where I was in the middle of a beautiful place and I was... I felt that I was overcome with joy and I ran down a slope and I felt totally alive, I suppose you would say, blissed out. I have never forgotten it. I wrote about it and kept it. I still have it. The experience has fed me and of course I have had many similar experiences since but the first was an awakening or perhaps even an enlightenment that has allowed me to return through the same gateway.

Karen: An intuition, since I can remember being able to read and articulate at 5 years old, so probably earlier, of "there's more than what our 5 senses tell us" coupled with "humans are 'more than' too". Then at about 12 or 13 I had my first unitive experience, triggered by a flower. I must have already been reading about these things as I clearly knew this was what is called a mystical experience, and that it was Divine in nature.

Chapter 2: Images, Ideas and Influences

I call this chapter 'Images, Ideas and Influences' partly to say something about the power of imagery. When contributors speak about ideas and influences that they now see as having weight in their adolescence and early adulthood, the ones that take root seem to be accompanied by vivid imagery and the feelings it evokes. This is how Joanna talks about her connection to the Druid name.

Joanna: I've always been a Druid. As a child, I didn't have a name for it. I loved and held a deep respect and reverence for nature – it had always been my teacher. I was fortunate enough to grow up on the edge of a little village in Quebec, Canada, with the endless tracks of forest that ran over the mountains and valleys as my guide. When I was in my teens, I started reading medieval fantasy books, and came across Druids in them – oh, how I wished that Druids still existed, I thought!

Joanna's account evokes the same sense of connectedness to nature reported by a number of people in Chapter 1. And, also as for others, her growing sense of reverence and connection doesn't have a name. The world of heightened imagery provided by fantasy literature eventually suggests a name and the powerful feeling of "oh how I wished that Druids still existed". And here we all are. I wonder how much wishing like that there has been, in the generations following World War 2, and just how much fantasy literature – an officially humble genre – has had to do with it. Certainly, there are other people in this group with something to say about books.

Books

Books are understood as having been important signposts to several people, pointing them both towards and away from possible destinations. Tom talks about ancient stories and modern interpretative frameworks.

Tom: What first drew me to Druidry were the old Welsh stories and English and Irish ... Irish mythology fascinated me back when I was in the US. So that sort of started me in this direction. And also my reading of Jung. And the *White Goddess*, although I know now that most of that has been made up – the poetry in it and what you sort of ... could see out of the corner of your eye - when reading that I knew it was part of what I was after. And then I started taking an online Druidry course with someone who has now become my wife, Nimue, and realised that this was what I had been doing in a solitary kind of way all along. Other people were identifying in this way.

Julie talks about the role of modern fantasy literature.

Julie: My spiritual wanderings took me in many directions, one of which was science-fantasy novels, particularly Stephen Donaldson's series *The Chronicles of Thomas Covenant, The Unbeliever.* In those I came across the idea of the land being 'alive' and people and other beings interacting with the energies of wood and stone and landscape. This felt wonderful; there was that rootedness in a land and interaction with the natural world, so although there is a lot more to the novels of the Thomas Covenant series, this is what stood out most for me at the time. Another book I read around that time and which was life-changing for me was Marion Bradley's *The Mists of Avalon*. This again introduced the idea of a sacred spirituality connected deeply to the land. I went off to explore Goddess spirituality and Wicca for a while then, as well as visiting Glastonbury for the first time. These spiritual paths felt a lot closer to what I was looking for but somehow still not quite 'it'.

I talk about poetry.

James: I remember when I was in my later teens sitting on a hillside quite close to the place where my father once went with me through the woods. I was reading Eliot's *Four Quartets* knowing that I lived within four miles of East Coker, for which one of the quartets is named, and where Eliot himself had been buried only a few years previously. And I was trying to get a sense of what they were saying. Something breathed itself into me even though I didn't exactly get it and couldn't clearly name what it was that I wasn't getting. There was something in the imagery that pointed to... possibilities.

Taken as a whole, Four Quartets was a step beyond me at 16. But individual sections had a great impact. For example I got a powerful image of how not to be in the depiction of city workers on the London tube "distracted from distraction by distraction". On the other side of the coin, I never forgot the section of Burnt Norton beginning: "At the still point of the turning world... At the still point, there the dance is" – leaving me to wonder at the abundant co-presence of stillness and dance as ultimate reality and so in some way my ultimate reality too. These images bypassed my ordinary thinking, which by this time had abandoned religion and in particular the Anglican Church, and reached my deepest intuition. But it didn't lead to any action at that time.

Important reading also includes more instructional kinds of spiritual literature, though literature relevant to the needs of this group hasn't always been easy to get hold of. For many of us, the on-line age developed well into our adult life times. Penny reminds us.

Penny: And reading a lot. But when I started taking an interest in spirituality before my teenage years there were no non-fiction books whatsoever. There were two Doreen Valiente books in the local library and there were books on Atlantis and Lemuria. . Nothing else. And then of course go forward 15 years and there are books by R. J. Stewart, Caitlin and John Matthews, Gareth Knight, all these sorts of people: and books by the Farrars, which I read with great interest; they taught me I didn't want to be a Witch. So I knew more about what I didn't want to be rather than what I did want to be. I loved Dion Fortune's books. I thought about the Western Mystery tradition. But then it appeared to me that that was basically mystical Christianity. And I knew I didn't want Christianity. So, there were various stages of exploration for me, as the teachers of the 1950s – 1970s got their publishing contracts and the way gradually opened up for everyone to explore more native beliefs and indigenous practice: and eventually I found the OBOD course, through my teacher.

Katy: In my first professional job I was a cataloguer for Dorset County Library Service. Many new books crossed my desk and so I got to see a lot of literature that wouldn't have come my way normally. This was in the mid-1980s. One book was Janet and Colin Farrar's *The Witch's Way* which with my folklorist's hat on I found fascinating. It was the section about beliefs and attitudes that I found most attractive – I have to say getting my kit off for ritual did not appeal ... I wondered how to get in touch with people like these, but at that time it wasn't so easy to find Pagan magazines and groups, and so it went on the back burner for about 20 years – just there in the background while I got on with other things.

But for Joanna, at a somewhat later period, things are already easier.

Joanna: When I was in college I found Wicca through a pagan shop in Montreal, where I picked up a copy of Scott Cunningham's *Wicca: A Guide for the Solitary Practitioner*. I practiced my own form of Wicca for a while.

People

Two of the group report being strongly influenced by individuals in early life. At the end of her teens, Eve is taken out of her usual surroundings to become an au pair for an Icelandic artist living in France. Robert talks about the inspiration provided by his grandmother with her traditional country views of life, still essentially Pagan in this account.

Eve: When I was about 18 or 19, I was an au pair girl and went to France, and there was an Icelandic woman I was working for. And she was an artist and she made these wonderful ritualistic figures, Icelandic and Nordic figures. So that was an incredible experience to meet someone who translated her experience, history and culture into such a powerful medium.

Robert: My Grandmother was a great inspiration in my life, from a generation that knew the ways of the land, when to plant things, little charms and recipes that would both elevate or heal a weary soul. These were just old country ways, passed on to her by her Mother; it was the stuff that was essential to living a good life. She would make cough syrups for winter and lemonades for summer and once in a while she would offer a little something to the fairies at the bottom of the garden, 'just to keep the balance' she would say. She evoked within me a world of magic and mystery where everything was possible, where fairies did live at the bottom of the garden and elves in the house and once in a while, to keep them happy, you propitiated them.

But personal inspiration can come at later stages in the journey as well. Two other contributors pay specific tribute to the inspiration of Emma Restall Orr (Bobcat).

Mark: Toward the end of the last millennium, I was driving somewhere for work and was captured by a piece on radio 4, for which I have a deep affection. I'd previously discounted Druidry as a valid path because of the preconceptions of old men in white sheets and fake beards prancing around Stonehenge. I'd been to the old Stonehenge festivals but I'd been far too ... chilled to notice any sort of sacred practice there. But this radio presenter was interviewing a Druidess, Emma Restall Orr, and made a comment about her not wearing white. She laughed and said something like, "of course not, out here in the landscape it'd get filthy; you'd never wash all the mud out" (or blood, I may have misheard and she does have some wit), "and think of all the bleach needed to keep it white."

From then, I had a different perspective on Druidry; not patriarchal, environmentally conscious, and linking in to the sacred inspirited landscape. I joined a few message boards, joined the BDO just as Philip Shallcrass took it into hibernation and, following an email conversation with Emma, joined the newly fledged TDN. I listened to that radio programme and that single interview put me on a line with Druidry. Not the Druidry of the white cloak and the staff and all the rest of it. But the Druidry of wandering in the woods – perhaps a little bit, you know cloaked, blending in and being a part of, and enacting a Druidry which was basically being in the natural world and experiencing it.

Beyond a brief foray into the OBOD and BDO correspondence courses, which proved how I don't work well in structured learning situations, I've never really looked anywhere else. My impression of the word Druid is a verb; Druid is what you do, not who you are, and I am content with that.

Karen: I wasn't attracted to the forms of Druidry available in the 80s, when I knew David and Peter Loxley. Bobcat's *Druid Priestess* fell off a bookshelf at my feet 10 years ago, I opened it, read a single passage and knew this was the 'name' of the path I was already on – if this was Druidry, then I'm a Druid, and have been in previous lives.

Said simply, Bobcat's version of Druidry gave shape and language to the animist sensibility which I'd only found before in Taoism (which had been good, yet not quite 'it'). Bobcat herself restored to me my ability and faith in my non-ordinary sensing which I had almost suppressed and learnt to treat with scepticism for a decade or two. I shared with her perceptions and unsought past life memories relating specifically to her, and she validated all of them. What a gift – having one's sight restored. This is relevant because it, together with experiences on or as a result of workshops with her allowed me to validate myself as a member of the Druid community, and also as having a direct and personal relationship with the land, the forest, the wind. A two-way relationship, not simply loving them as human to 'it'.

Broader cultural influences

Both JJ and Mark were supported by positive trends and influences in the general culture and associated with the words "hippy" and "hippiedom". For JJ this leads to a defined spiritual question and learning from a variety of traditions. Whatever he has gained from other paths, most notably Buddhism, he describes always coming home to a Western Way rootedness in the land. Mark speaks of psychedelic music, sunsets and a "gentle questing for connection barely understood at the time". And Nimue describes multiple influences, from Pagan oriented parents, from her grandmother's relationship to landscape, and from the discovery of existentialism at college. The result is a Druidry characterised by a concern with "the issues about meaning, and the absence of meaning, and the necessity of making your own".

JJ: I don't know, hippiedom was a religion in a way for a while, "make love not war" – and so all through that and then searching through Shamanism, Buddhism, Hinduism – no, not Hinduism - Shamanism, Sufism, and the Western Mystery tradition ... and Buddhism. Western Mysteries. That was very much part of my emergence – Hermetic Gnosticism: which are words where most people say, "Well, what are you on about?" ... the mystery of magic, the mystery of the unknown, of not knowing. But what I love about Western, what's important to me, is about being related and rooted in this land. Buddhism has been very important to me for years, but as a feeder, and as a bed partner to the Druidry in a sense. But it doesn't do it completely for me without other elements.

Mark: In my early teens I was very taken with the hippy culture that had been and gone before me, and in some of the ideas of a merged hippy/technology lifestyle. I spent time listening to psychedelic music and watching the sun rise and set. In the lack of the word Awen I guess I was gently questing for a connection barely understood at the time.

Nimue: Existentialism I stumbled into by accident in college, and the issues about meaning, and the absence of meaning, and the necessity of making your own were really important for me. Paganism – my parents were dabbling in it when I was a child, so it was on my radar. And it was my grandmother talking about her relationship with landscape as a spiritual issue in my early teens that really got me looking that way. And realising that there was something to look for. I joined the Pagan Federation at 18 and it just rattled along from there. And when I found Druids it was just kind of obvious that that was where I fitted. And I'd been doing quite a lot of it anyway. I just didn't know that that was what it was called.

Churches

Several of us have had Christian-influenced upbringings, since Christianity was and remains the dominant spiritual tradition in Britain and North America where all the interviewees grew up (13 and 2 respectively). So it's worth saying something about ways in which churches both were and weren't influential in our formative years. (Positive adult encounters with the Christian tradition, when people were already Druids, will be described later in this book.)

Responses range from an experience of Pentecostalism that was oppressive (Mark) to one of Unitarianism that was empty (Tom).

Mark: In the mid Seventies, they *[Mark's mother and stepfather]* became attached to a church in Bristol renowned for being a bit 'happy clappy', and from that point their Pentecostal journey began, and accelerated rapidly. For me the message was counterintuitive to the understandings I was coming to, and in fact the full-on day-long never-ending 'you must embrace Jesus' inevitably became a catalyst for me to begin examining exactly where my own spirituality lay; and it wasn't in the dogma and judgement of a Christian theology. It was a difficult home for me, as their new found religion expanded into every corner. My mother is now housebound but has preached gospel all over the world including in Pakistan surrounded by armed guards; this wasn't a simple church lifestyle they chose...And not only hard for me; my younger brother eventually moved in with a friend's family to get away.

Tom: Then as I got older, my family had a rule that you had to go to church on Sunday. They did not specify which church. They simply said that you had to go to church. So I went to pretty much every available church in my home town and became very cynical of organised religion as a result of this. I ended up settling on the Unitarian church because they did not seem to have any certain answers as to what was happening. But I became increasingly almost horrified by the giant vacuum this left. In being so all-inclusive, they seemed to be pointing at nothing – which was an idea that made me very, very uncomfortable and did not align with my experiences at all, which was that there definitely is something.

Three people – Katy, JJ and Penny – report enjoying some aspects of Church practice and community, but reject the path overall. There is some positive imagery, some cultural value, but it cannot prevail against an overall lack of connection with the Christian faith. Penny says that while "a waft of incense ... could bring "shivers down my back", High Anglicanism "could in no way fulfil my expectations".

Katy: I grew away from church-going when I spent a year in France as part of my degree course, and discovered I didn't enjoy church when I didn't know the hymns – I realised it was the singing that I liked above all. I found C. of E. ritual pretty meaningless – not helped by one particular vicar who read the liturgy as if it was a shopping list – and so gradually fell away from church and all mainstream religion.

JJ: Catholicism as a child, which has resonance... and although I rejected it at 13 or thereabouts in that department, because at that time ... the lack of honouring the feminine, lack of respect for the earth ...meant it didn't hit the spot ... however in terms of ritual and incense and candles and that, it does have something ...

Penny: My father was High Anglican. And what I loved were the bells and smells. And so there was the nature connection I felt intuitively, and also the sense of Mystery that the

Church opened me up to but could in no way fulfil my expectations. I didn't get anything from the Church services but those adjuncts to the service that brought shivers down my back when I got a waft of incense.

Two people, Nimue and I, parted company with the Church of England largely on intellectual grounds, unconvinced by the way in which major questions were handled.

Nimue: I think it was the desire for it was there from the very beginning of my life, although I went through Sunday school and a Church of England School, and they just didn't answer it at all. But the questions about why we are here, what is it for, what happens when we die. I can't remember a time when I wasn't thinking about that. And I was sent to a Sunday school at four because I kept asking awkward questions.

James: I was getting mixed messages from the circles in which I found myself as a questing young teenager. Intellectually it was OK to know that the Bible was a diverse book from diverse cultural periods. And it was likewise OK (I'm talking about the mid-1960s) to think that the Christian tradition had over-emphasised transcendence at the expense of immanence, and to entertain a view of the Divine as ground of being rather than Supreme Being. But it was also understood that these were minority views within the Church and, although accepted as valid for debate, in my world they were not associated with an alternative set of practices. The services stayed the same. The liturgy stayed the same. Petitionary prayer stayed the same.

Julie says that she "worked at" Christianity "pretty hard", but "never felt anything more than an outsider". The Christianity she tended to encounter was unhealthily ascetic and to the extent that she felt an attraction to this, it was an attraction to resist.

Julie: I think I've always been interested in spirituality really. Early in my life I was exposed mostly to Christianity which I worked at pretty hard but I realise that I never felt anything more than an outsider. I just didn't 'believe' the things one is expected to believe as a Christian, and I've come to the conclusion that 'belief' isn't something wholly under ones conscious control. The type of Christianity I seemed to repeatedly encounter appeared to applaud extreme actions (such as living up a pole for thirty-seven years, or avoiding sleep and/or food for days at a time) and that wasn't a good ideal for me to be aiming at. I could be quite good at some types of extreme behaviour, such as avoiding food, but that clearly wasn't a healthy place to be at all. Christianity as I encountered it then also felt very bleak and rather misogynistic.

David describes himself as "a Devotional Hellenic Polytheist" and says that his path remains "nature centred" even though no longer "Celtic". Overall his use of language gives me the sense of an internal continuity of spiritual life and practice despite major shifts in allegiance. More than anyone else in this group, he seems at ease with his earlier Christian path, active well into adult life. The watchword for this continuity is 'active spirituality'.

David: If the terms 'Celtic' and 'Druidry' are held to be inseparable, then I'm not a Druid by that definition. If by 'Druidry' is meant 'nature centred' or 'nature focused', then I am both a Druid and a Hellenist. Druidry entered my life in October 2008 and at that point was Celtic in its character. Since then my own spirituality has developed further, but the aspects of being nature-focused and –conscious still remain.

I've been interested in spiritual life, mostly all of my life, from Sunday school as a child (not my choice!), through church choirs, then membership in its own right, a couple of decades in the New Churches in the 70s to early 90s, then as an Anglican deacon and Benedictine Oblate. Thereafter, despite having ended my association with the Church of England, 'active spirituality' continues to be something which I believe to be central to my self-identity and practice.

Chapter 3: Questing and Discovery

Chapters 3 and 4 are about arrival – how people have established their mature spiritual identities. For many, this has been in the embrace of Druidry, and Chapter 4 deals with that. But for a significant section of this group, something that seems like their major imprint has occurred before their entry into Druidry and therefore significantly flavours, or informs, or to an extent qualifies their Druidry itself. Six stories from the interviews particularly bring this out.

The first is from Elaine, who recounts a major spiritual awakening and how she follows it up. A powerful energetic awakening in a magical landscape precipitates "a dissolving of my ego and then it being reformed again". This comes with a message: "honour the Goddess", a message that guides her in her subsequent journey.

Elaine: In my twenties and thirties I became very interested humanistic psychology and I attended a variety of personal growth workshops. The most significant of these was a residential workshop I went to in 1983 called *The Awakening Journey* at CAER (the Centre for Alternative Education and Research) in Cornwall. During this workshop, triggered by accident rather than design I had an intense experience which according to my later research fits the description of a kundalini awakening. It was quite frightening at the beginning when I felt something move and unwind at the base of my spine, release itself by flying up through my body and annihilating me in the process.

For a while I was outside of Space and Time, I have no memory of what happened during this time but I do remember my experience of returning from the Void. It was like watching a reverse recording of mirror that has been shattered and seeing the pieces reform again. I was hugely relieved and jubilant to have come back together again and to have survived my annihilation. I was different after this. In the short term for the next day or so I became clairvoyant and in the longer term I had an insight into the energy emanating from all things. I also came back with a message which was "Honour the Goddess".

At that time this was very pertinent to me as I was a feminist who could not see the divine feminine reflected in any of the mainstream religions. I became aligned with feminist, Goddess spirituality and Dianic Witchcraft. I felt very inspired by Starhawk's Spiral Dance and the art of Monica Sjoo. I would say that's where I came in, although after a while I decided I didn't just want to be a separatist and I looked for a group of people who were working with both men and women. I was initiated into British Traditional Wicca and that was a home for me and gave me some fellow travellers. With a group of peers I've worked in a Wiccan and a neo-Shamanic style in the past. I've always been a bit of a fusion person and these have been exciting and creative years for me being involved with many neo-Pagan and magical groups creating spaces for certain types of human experience to be validated and named.

Eve talks about her apprenticeship with Starhawk and her subsequent work in Shamanism and women's ritual groups.

This is a powerful, intense and in some ways defining time. But there comes a process of revisioning and re-adjustment, and a shift in her spiritual centre of gravity. Eventually she becomes a Priestess of Brighid under the aegis of Caitlin Matthews, and subsequently enrols on the OBOD distance learning course. Here the Ovate course in particular is a homecoming – not so much through providing new material, but in allowing a reflective reprise of her spiritual life to date.

Eve: I used to go to Witch Camp and I was apprenticed to Starhawk. And Starhawk was very important to me. Being in the landscape, and doing ritual in the landscape, it was a very powerful, intense time. In a sense when – moving on many years – I put all of that down, it was because I found it didn't suit my true essence. The power and intensity of working with ritual somehow was too brightly coloured for me. And it's quite a sensitive subject because I got my fingers burnt a few times. I was working with a Shamanic, Native American Shaman at the time. Some of what happened felt brutal and unkind.

So I had to, over a period of 10 years I think, in my 30s and early 40s, I had to look very carefully at what I had been part of. And so, also my 30s and 40s I was involved with starting a Moon Group. And we had some very powerful experiences in that. We worked with the 8 festivals of the year... and we always had a ritual and performed that together and I can remember some quite intense, extreme rituals which others felt drawn to act out and I felt, actually, I wouldn't have done that. I remember a stabbing of something at Lammas, I didn't do it, but someone else did it – the stabbing of the corn, of the bread king. Things like that which, you know, I found, extreme and frightening even. I think it goes right back to a very, very sensitive, psychic child, who needed quite a lot of protection and boundaries around herself.

I don't think I've said enough about Caitlin Matthews - she brought Brighid to me. Somehow the celebration of Imbolc was a key experience. I did a lot of inner work. That was my favourite festival. I felt very connected to Her. I did an initiation ceremony where I became a Priestess of Brighid and I think where I naturally sit is with a Bright Brighid energy, Brighid as Goddess of the Land. The Imbolc rituals, the songs, the crafting of a celebration of the land in its different seasons came from what I learnt from Caitlin. This led to Druidry. I found out about OBOD from Rosa and decided to do it. The material wasn't new to me I was finding a home, I guess, finding a home that felt very held ... Most particularly the Ovate year resonated. A mixture of ancestral work, trees, herbs, animals. I had had an herb garden and harvested herbs in my 20s. Since my 20s I had known the common names of wild flowers that were my friends. The Ovate course brought important strands of my life together in a very contained way. What had been missing was giving my creativity a form apart from being a psychotherapist. Working with textiles and embroidery emerged from that year.

For Robert the situation is a little different. He too has immersed himself in powerful traditions − Witchcraft, Peruvian Shamanism and the Tibetan Bon tradition. Yet, as he presents his journey, the most powerful teacher is illness. The work of engaging with OBOD Druidry - and creating a contemplative Druidry informed by the Bon tradition is the result of hard days, incapacity and eventual surrender.

Robert: As I got older I discovered Witchcraft. The forces of nature had coalesced into anthropomorphic forms and into the guises of The God and The Goddess who I met as equals under the canopy of the trees. I found a definition for the things that fed my soul. I came to Druidry through the myths of the land but this happened much later in life. I had already studied with a Peruvian Shaman and spent ten years taking teachings from a Lama from the Bon tradition. My spiritual path was well developed and then suddenly I became ill, it happened almost overnight and for two years I was bedridden. All I knew was washed away leaving me suspended in an empty place cut off from the world. Those were hard days, friends dwindled away and after a few years of incapacity I realised that the life I had known had gone. Beliefs, success, career, money, status, were gone. With no more masks to hide behind, I was laid bare, I thought I was going to die, so I surrendered and let go.

Rosa's journey has been highly influenced by Christian tradition. Her connection with this tradition does not come from childhood – her parents were atheists. It came after awakening and exploration in adulthood (Rosa mentions Buddhism, Siddha Yoga, Ramana's self-inquiry and Native American journeying), early in her mid-life period. The catalyst was the Anglican priest and mystic Eric Pyecroft and has involved an embrace of elements in Christian tradition without taking on orthodox Christian doctrines.

Rosa: Joining OBOD felt like a homecoming, and since that time Druidry has become the overall container for my practice. Since the mid-1970s I have explored Buddhism, Siddha Yoga and Ramana's self-inquiry as well as Native

American journeying, combined with a great deal of therapeutic work of various kinds.

In the 80s I learned a great deal about contemplative meditation from a remarkable C. of E. vicar called Eric Pyecroft. I sat with him many times a week for several years. He ran meditation groups in his church and in the 'cowshed' at his home. I was baptised and confirmed at that time by Eric, although I did not consider myself a Christian and had issues with much of the Church's teaching.

Four years ago I read a book called *The Way of the Practical Mystic*, a correspondence course written in the 1920s by Henry Hamblin and recently republished. His approach to Christianity enabled me to fully embrace Jesus' teaching, much of it not in the Bible! Recently I have been studying Rudolph Steiner, and I now work with his *Calendar of the Soul* and *Foundation Stone* meditation. I use Ceile De prayer beads and practice as a basis for my meditation. Casting a circle to create a Druid Sacred Grove holds together all these threads.

The fifth story describes my awakening through transpersonal psychology, which in at least some iterations is esoteric spirituality under another name. The context is a therapy training, in a broadly Jungian tradition, but the major effect on me is in the spiritual domain, which I attribute partly to my teachers and partly to an internal readiness. In the same period I discovered R. J. Stewart and worked in particular with his Merlin material. This gave me a practice but not a home. So I found my way to OBOD. But the neo-Gnostic vision of my earlier training has meant that concern with land, ancestors and indigenous tradition does not wholly define my spiritual path. There are other dimensions too.

James: I became wholeheartedly involved in named spiritual life and practice well into adulthood. I was prompted by a personal journey through humanistic and transpersonal psychology, the world of growth groups, counselling and therapy. I was specifically studying with Ian Gordon-Brown and Barbara Summers at the London Transpersonal Centre. They were largely Jungian in orientation, though they also drew on Psychosynthesis and Gestalt models. Ian had once worked for the Lucis Trust founded by Alice Bailey, and Barbara had worked with refugees from the Tibetan monastic diaspora. They became the catalysts for a sea-change in the way I perceived and experienced the world. My centre of gravity shifted and I experienced life that little bit differently. The key years were 1987-1991, for me a classical mid-life period (aged 37-42).

During my time with the Transpersonal Centre I connected with the work of Bob Stewart. I was drawn into his work with old Scottish border ballads, particularly *Thomas the Rhymer* and *Tam Lin.* The theme was universal – the underworld journey – but the ballads were specifically grounded in Celtic Faerie tradition. My father's family came from that part of the world – he was born in Selkirk – and that I think was part of the attraction. So that and other writings of Bob Stewart kicked me off: his *Way of Merlin* work, particularly *The Mystic Life of Merlin,* based substantially around a story from Dumfriesshire, still in the border area though further to the west. These were local stories with a universal resonance. In more recent years the last section of *The Mystic Life of Merlin*, where Merlin and a small group of companions form a contemplative community in the Caledonian Forest, helped to confirm me in my own contemplative turn.

The London Transpersonal Centre encouraged an interest in the traditions of India, Tibet and China as well as the spiritual heritage of the west. Within the latter, I began reading Nag Hammadi literature and appreciated aspects of Christian Gnosticism as well as Celtic and Arthurian tradition, grail seeking tradition, nearer to home. I might describe my overall view at that time as neo-Gnostic: affirming of world, body and senses, whilst also engaged with the inner life of the psyche, and alerted to the value of contemplative illumination. I carried these interests with me into OBOD.

Finally, Joanna discusses her involvement with Zen Buddhism and what it has brought to her practice of Druidry. She has written about this in more detail elsewhere, in her book Zen Druidry.

Joanna: I think that Druidry sits well with pretty much any spiritual tradition. If the focus is a deep reverence and relationship with nature, then that works with anything. I studied Buddhism and Zen for a couple of years, which influences the way I think, the way I behave and certain practices that I adopted into my Druidry. As the Celts had Indo-European roots, there are very many similarities between the Dharmic traditions and Druidry – they work very well together. The eightfold path in Buddhism sits very well within Druidry, offering guidelines as to how to create honourable relationship in the world from a human context. So do the four noble truths, and the five precepts. Druidry then influences those principles, using nature as inspiration

– it forms an endless circle of Awen (see my first book, *Zen Druidry*, for more).

The deep love for nature and the creation of an honourable relationship with the natural world has formed the basis of my Druidry ever since I can remember. I've always communed with nature, feeling my soul blend in with my environment, wanting to learn more about it and where I fit into the cycle. The values of learning from your environment, of finding your place and living in balance and harmony, have shaped every aspect of my Druidry. It has given me a language with which I can express what I have always felt about the natural world.

Chapter 4: Druid Identity and Values

Druid Identity

Druids may be diverse in their beliefs and practices and eclectic in disposition. Many have had a long and varied journey before finding their Druid path. Yet Druid identities are strong, articulated with passion and devotion, though without a neat uniformity. I present six statements which touch on Druid identity and what it means to the people concerned. The contributors are: Nimue, Tom, JJ, Julie, James, Penny.

Nimue: A big consolidation process for me, when I did the Bardic Grade of OBOD. That was really the process of realising how all the various strands in my life actually made a coherent sense that I'd never seen before. So I was about 25 or 26 when I was doing that, recently a parent, trying to find out who I was and where I fitted. And working through the Bardic Grade and finding that the music and the poetry and the interest in folklore and the landscape stuff and all the natural stuff and the activism – everything, everything that I was drawn to, it was all part of this same coherent unified thing that is Druidry. And that was, that was a very wild period for me, because every time the Gwersi came through the door it was like, 'bloody hell, another one'. And that was a fantastic process. So that sense of coming together as a whole entity rather than a lot of loosely connected fragments, that was a big part of how I started out.

At various times various bits of it become more important to me than others. That seems to be very fluid and that can be one year to the next, one month to the next. Depends on what external life brings, really. All of it – be it more at the fore or more at the back, depending on what happens.

Tom: I would say Druidry as I understand it describes and encompasses everything that I'm doing. I don't really need to reach outside of it because it does have lovely malleable borders, but as I perceive it something at the centre, making it different from the Unitarian experience. And I would say that the only other thing that I have any sort of name for is probably still within the confines of Druidry and that there's an element I would say of something like Shamanism in what I do, which is not in any way separate from the rest of my life, I would say.

JJ: I came to a point of thinking that I would have to forge my own path, and then, how long ago would that be, 25 years I think, I came across OBOD and Druidry. And like many people, like most people, it felt like coming home. It was on the same wavelength and it hit the right note in relation to the earth and this land. And the elements. And it just 'did it' ... so I came into through the course, but then met up with people at a Grove in Bristol: - 1994 was the first time I went, it must have been 1994.

I went to my first Grove meeting, the same 'first meeting' that both Adrian Rooke and Ronald Hutton went to. The three of us ... we all came from nowhere, in that moment, together, and have become lifetime friends through that. So there is a certain synchronicity there but also, as I look on it, it changed my life ... it seems there's loads that I could say. First of all in terms of the course I love the – I would call it, in the Bardic, a flowering into oneself, but in a 'thy' sense – a flowering unto thine self in the Bardic, for me. And creative and music and poetry but flowering.

Then the Ovate, diving deep into shadowland, ancestors and trees – in a way, really rich soil but also difficult territory in a way, it throws up stuff, but then bringing it all home with Druidry. You know, putting it into practice. The path is one of work, worship, service; that's one of the Druid triads – *Hearth as Altar, Work as Worship, Service as Sacrament* – that's a guiding light for me. Within the wider community, then as part of Silurian grove, which then became the Dobunni. This has been a strong grove and a powerful one. I mean like anywhere, characters come and go and not everybody always gels - a rich mix, and each seed group or grove will have its own flavour. I'm still part of that. I left for a while and then came back in recent years.

And then there's camps, through community and through ritual practice. I look at it now and in a field long ago I was asked to do a hand fasting. Somebody recognised something in me and through that, my life, gradually, I've developed the skills in that environment and took them out into the world to do ritual, to do handfastings and namings and parting ceremonies. They are part of my life. My life has become what was ... yeah what was opened up as potential has become reality for me.

Julie: I read *Elements of the Druid Tradition* by Philip Carr-Gomm and *The Book of Druidry* by Ross Nichols and signed up for the OBOD correspondence course. I was on my spiritual way! There was the ancient heritage and connection to this land of Britain, and the deep connection with the natural world; this was what I had been looking for! I can honestly say that I've never looked back.

My only regret was that I had a deep yearning to be part of a contemplative religious community and Druidry didn't seem to have that. I developed my own contemplative practice from what I was learning in the OBOD course, particularly the (old) Ovate Grade, and for many years thought that as far as being a contemplative Druid was concerned I was in a minority of one! Indeed, many Pagans I'd met had seemed very against any type of Druid or Pagan monastic practice, so I simply developed and followed my own contemplative/monastic Druid practice as a solitary for many years. I did work with London Grove (now Tamesis Seedgroup) for some years and I really enjoyed that and certainly learned a lot, so I wasn't a completely solitary solitary.

I carried on with my daily contemplative practice and joined The Daughters of the Flame, and the Sisterhood of Avalon as well and although I'm not deeply involved with the Sisterhood at this stage it was through a link in a post on their Yahoo Group that I came across a website with the words 'Monastic Druidry' in it. This I just had to investigate, and this was how I found the Order of the Sacred Nemeton (OSN) which is a contemplative Druid Order and with which I work mostly nowadays. I was overjoyed to find that I wasn't in a minority of one after all! It's true that monastic Druids are certainly in a minority in the Druid community as a whole, and I think that will always be the case. Most religions do have a 'monastic stream' and it is always only a minority of people who want to, or feel called to, work in that way with their spirituality. I'm so happy to have found the OSN! It really does feel like my spiritual home.

James: When I entered OBOD in 1993 I liked the recognition given to its early modern period. It gave Druidry a place to stand within the emergence of modernity and its big questions. Druidry's re-appearance coincides with a point in the eighteenth century when the age of reason, for some people at least, was finding its heart, articulating a new understanding of 'nature' and stumbling towards a belief in universal human rights. People were also developing a more Universalist frame of reference, taking an interest in the traditions of other parts of the globe even while colonising and exploiting them. I see the beginnings of the culture I belong to, actually a culture of tremendous contradictions: but mine, anyway. Druidry connects with that culture and its development as well as celebrating an older past. We draw on all our inheritance – from archaic Shamanism to the 21st century, bracing for an unknown future. So there is that sense of the whole tree of tradition, rooted in the earliest times and still growing today.

Penny Every new spiritual movement has its egrigore – an inner reality made up not only of the ideas of the members, but also the invisible influences from the other realms that resonate with that `flavour' of spiritual thought; and as Druids we are dedicated to making connections not only in the natural world but on the other planes as well, other states of consciousness. So you could say that every grade of Druidry has an inner Grove. I think for groups of people who are practising together, it's of huge value to have quiet time together, to allow the space for that. I think the inner Grove of Druidry will pour down blessings on the people who are incarnate at the moment if we allow that time and space. And contemplating on that aspect of Druidry together stops Druids falling into the personality trap, which I think they can do. We're not there to like each other on a personal level. We're there to do Druid work together and to respect each other because we're on the same path. I mean hopefully we're a bunch of pleasant people and will like each other as well. That's a bonus. But if we don't, everyone's got a right to be there. But certainly if there's certainly a feeling that a group is starting to form, being quiet together in some sort of guided way can really help develop that egrigore. And the same thing happens when we allow that quiet time when the whole Order comes together, Philip always does a visualisation with us all. Very, very important.

Druid Values

The interviews and written responses included a number of powerful statements about Druid values. I present six of them – from Robert, Julie, Katy, Tom, Mark and Joanna.

For Robert, Druidry is a label (and not the only one) which points to "the unity in each other ... the same essence behind each person's eyes". It also points to the planet we live on, and the force of love. Values come out of these recognitions.

Robert: Druidry like any other word is a label to define something. I practice Druidry and also practice other traditions; to me they all have the same flavour. I have spent time with a Peruvian Shaman, a Tibetan Lama and what they teach in essence is the same as Druidry. It's about connecting, finding a place within where we can peacefully abide. Druidry is the planet we live upon. We are humanity in its many different faces and when we see the unity in each other, see that same essence behind each person's eyes, that's where I find my Druidry. Druidry aims to find a light within to navigate the pathways of the soul. That light is at the heart of all spiritualities and there is one word that defines it: love.

So my Druidry is about love, it's about loving the land I live upon, it's about loving nature, loving my brothers and sisters and also loving myself. Druidry can help us to laugh and find joy, when you find those things then stay there, kind friends and family, community and the ability to be generous with our time are the greatest gifts that we can ever search for. These things are all at the heart of Druidry, allowing everyone to come together and find a place that is real.

Julie points to Druidry's hopeful, optimistic world view in which "nothing is wasted, no experience is irrelevant; one can learn from anything". She celebrates Druidry's inclusive and non-judgemental nature, non-hierarchical stance and a sense of the "equality of all beings".

Julie: What particularly stands out for me is that rooted connection to the land and the reverence for the natural world. I had grown up loving nature so following a spiritual path which leaves nature out, or labels it as evil, wasn't going to work for me; it felt wrong.

As far as the role it has played is concerned, I can honestly say that without it I may not still have been here. I have had a lot of health problems over the last couple of decades and Druidry has brought a more hopeful, more optimistic worldview than some other spiritualities which see suffering as 'all one's own fault', or 'the result of evil actions in former lives so one deserves it'. Druidry brings to me the idea that nothing is wasted, no experience is irrelevant; one can learn from everything. This has certainly helped me, and it is something I try to impart to prisoners I now work with in my capacity as a Pagan Prison Chaplain. There is in Druidry no sense that anyone is 'damned forever', and this certainly brings me hope. The non-judgmental stance is one that I particularly value, as well as the inclusivity and equality of all beings. The non-hierarchical stance is also a breath of fresh air, and something I think human society needs right now.

Katy and Tom both emphasise Druidry's tolerance and freedom, with Tom adding his sense of "bringing the possibility of what you find, and making it manifest in the world in a responsible sort of a way".

Katy: The values I cherish most are those of tolerance and freedom to craft my own path. Of course these are aspirations in the tradition – I've met people who tried to force me to fit in with them and who couldn't tolerate difference (one reason why I find groups difficult) – but generally freedom to find one's own way is built into Druidry. We are given a structure and then left free to work within it, changing it to make it right for us.

Tom: Probably the values are what attract me most. And the possibility of bringing what you find, and making it manifest in the world in a responsible sort of a way. I had no idea of what to expect, in terms of community. And all of that has been an extremely pleasant surprise. I don't think I could have imagined anything quite this good, actually, on my own before I got here. Because there were no Druids that I was aware of in the U.S. The non-judgemental freedom to explore ideas and beliefs. The sense of easy spiritual camaraderie and lack of unnecessary structure. There is no one Druid ritual. There is no one Druid way of doing things. So, the support in exploration, I would say.

Mark explains how "working with truth leads us to living an honourable life", in the context of a path emphasising "mud, blood and heritage". And Joanna talks about "truth, honour, service" and says, "A Druid's life is one lived in service to the greater whole, as is each living thing – the oak provides oxygen, it lives in service by being true to its nature and singing its soul song in freedom".

Mark: Working with truth leads us to living an honourable life. Honour is simply the courage to live. I find it's a simple way to refer to the way I view the Druid path, or mine at least. It's Mud, Blood and Heritage.

The Mud is all about the geographic landscape in which you are based. The Blood is your family lineage. And the Heritage is the story of Druidry. My Mud is the Severn Vale of southern Gloucestershire. I was born in Bristol and have seldom lived far from it, currently living in a village between Bristol and Stroud. Everything about the landscape; the hills, the streams, the views across to the Welsh mountains and the Cotswold Escarpment, and of course the wonderful sinuous river Severn ... these are essential parts of my world. Take me away, even quite a short distance away, and I am unsettled.

The Blood is family, genetic heritage ... the reason I have this nose and these eyes. Blood is important. It's who you are. It's your ancestry. It's where you came from. If you don't really know where you came from you don't really know which way you're pointed. My father died when I was six and my family moved away from Suffolk and I lost connection with that part of my blood. I've re-made a lot of that connection through genealogy, getting in contact and visiting and things like that. I've found a lot of interesting stuff about me in finding out about my relatives.

And then there's the Heritage, and that's the Druid Heritage: The stories that have survived and the stories that have been reinvented, and indeed the stories that are even now being invented. You can find the same truths in terms within many of the tales of our lands handed down through the generations. Very little of current Druid knowledge is really much more than a couple of hundred years old. And it's probably all the better for that. That heritage thing is really a shared community resource ...that's the third leg of the stool if you will. The Mud, the Blood and the Heritage.

Joanna: For me Druidry comes down the three things: truth, honour and service. When I speak of truth, I speak of each individual thing living in accordance to its true nature, and thereby living in harmony with the planet. We are all co-existing on this marvellous sphere. We evolved to do so. The world (humanity) can try to change our truth, however it is up to us to rediscover it should we stray from our true selves and our place in the world.

Through a life lived in truth and with honour, we immediately realise that by doing so we are serving the world. A Druid's life is one lived in service to the greater whole, as is each living thing – the oak provides oxygen, it lives in service by being true to its nature and singing its soul song in freedom. So do can we do the same when we realise our place in the world. In doing so, we can truly become the drui, those that have the wisdom of the oak.

Part 2: Practice

Introduction

Discussions of practice centre on four principle areas: formal sitting meditations; being in nature, walking the land; group practice and life practice; and Awen.

Levels of commitment to sitting practice vary. People can meditate solo, in groups or (in the case of Daily Offices) solo yet with a sense of other people participating. In most cases, formal meditation is seen as a resource for living with more awareness. Three kinds of sitting meditation are practised: visualisation and pathworking; Buddhist-influenced meditations; Daily Offices. Some of them, especially the last, shade into contemplative prayer. No-one in this group is turning their face from the world or trying to get off it. So there is no contradiction between this kind of practice and practices that involve engaging with nature or other people or being in the flow of everyday life. Unsurprisingly for a group of Druids, being in nature and creative arts are significant sites of contemplative practice – as is working to engage mindfully in groups and in the wider world.

The chapter on Awen looks at different views of Awen amongst contributors, and in particular a tendency by some people to extend Awen to cover resourceful contemplative states as well as its more traditional associations with poetic and vatic inspiration. The chapter identifies a broad range of opinion, and its implications, particularly concerning this use of that term in a contemplative context, are taken up in the final section of this book, *Reflections and Conclusions.*

Chapter 5: Formal Sitting Meditations

Visualisation and Pathworking

The classic Western Way approach to meditation is here described by Penny. It has a strong focus on visualisation and pathworking and tends to take up relatively short periods of time. In the form of the sacred grove and light body practices (especially when taken together) this way of working features very strongly in the OBOD distance learning course. Penny's own practice relies on "simple techniques", practised "little and often".

Penny: Well, the purpose of meditation for me is to keep me keyed in to my idea of being a spiritual being in a body, rather than just a body whizzing around in the mundane world. And I think we can do it with very simple techniques. Little and often is my motto. I'm not a natural contemplative in that it doesn't sit easily with me to sit for hours. I don't engage so much with the Eastern idea of making the mind blank. I like the Western approach of simple visualisations, pictures to keep the front of the mind busy, if you like, and also to programme the mind into getting into a sense of stillness quickly. And I do something of that every day; sometimes just a breathing exercise. Sometimes Philip's tree exercise, which combines breath and movement, and then I'll do visualisations, being contemplative in the sense of using techniques to enter into a focused, relaxed space. Actually blanking out the world is not my natural way of engaging with stillness.

Other people - James, Rosa, Nimue, Elaine, Tom and Katy - also talk about Western Way meditation, both within OBOD and in other settings. Katy includes the point that 'visualisation' may in fact occur kinaesthetically, rather than through the visual sense itself.

James: When I was working in transpersonal psychology I was highly engaged in visualisation, inner world exploration and journeying. The OBOD sacred grove and light body practice came naturally to me, and remained important to my personal Druid practice. I particularly liked the way in which the subtle energy work of the light body wove together with the experience of the sacred grove, as both were deepened and developed over the course of my OBOD training. In many ways this work, dedicated and held within the mandala of the Druid circle and under the wing of the Order was, and remains, the foundation stone of my individual spiritual practice – more so than inputs from any other individual source. It's a method of working that allows the practitioner a great deal of freedom and can be approached in divergent ways. This is a tremendous strength as I discovered for myself as a practitioner and then for others, when I became an OBOD mentor.

Rosa: Well guided meditation has been a very powerful tool at various times, journeying meditation, and learning a lot about my own inner psyche through that. I did a brief guided journey last Friday at a workshop. And Pan in the forest said: "Your only task is to keep your heart clear". And that struck me really profoundly as that is what it is actually about. Meditation is a way of keeping my heart clear. And I was thinking about that last night. A clear heart is an open heart.

Nimue: I started very much with a sort of visualisation and pathworking orientated practice, because that's what I encountered at first, probably in my late teens. I'd been to some workshops. And the creative, narrative aspects of that were very appealing. And mostly that was very relaxation oriented.

Elaine: Mostly my form of meditation practice was an active imagination practice called Hermetics. It is a magical training and it starts off with building up the light body and opening up elemental doorways and exploring them. I've practised it both solo and in groups. Working with a group often intensifies my experience of meditation.

Tom: Before I came to England I used to meditate quite a bit of the time. I had a reconditioned shed that I had winterised, because this was Maine. And I lived a pretty hermit-like life there. I read and I drew and I had a job as well. But I'd come back and this was in the middle of the country and I would just think and read and walk and much of my life was just a kind of hermit's meditation. So much of what I'm doing now is still feeding off the experiences that I had then.

Katy: Essentially I work solo but enjoy meditating in a group when I can find one, as long as they do simple meditation. Journey-work in a group emphatically does not work for me – I'm not visual on the inner planes and I can't spend two minutes 'really looking at that tree' when all I can see is the back of my eyelids. I get the essence of the tree in a single non-visual glimpse, all of it, in detail. My 'vision' is in the form of non-visual subliminal sense-impressions, so my inner journeys are exactly that – journeys – I travel. I see nothing, but can describe what I encounter in visual terms and in some detail.

Buddhist influenced Meditations

I have chosen the term `Buddhist influenced` rather than the more generic `mindfulness` for the next group of meditations, because the people practicing this form of meditation are concerned with more than the techniques of bare attention meditation. To a greater or lesser extent, they have been influenced by the ideas of the Buddhist tradition as well. This context helps to explain why they are not satisfied with traditional Western Way methods alone. Eve makes the case particularly strongly.

Eve: So I think when it comes to quite recently, let's say around 8 years ago, I had a lot of illness in my family. Each member of my family had been seriously ill up until 3 years ago and my own health is often compromised. I often felt unhinged during that period – each time I felt that I needed something to hold me, something spiritual to hold me. I didn't feel that OBOD was enough. It wasn't enough. My eldest daughter, through her experience and illness, turned to Buddhism. And so I became very interested in her experiences and I did a lot of listening to Pema Chodron and Tara Brach particularly and mindfulness and meditation.

So I turned to that kind of Buddhism to hold me during this difficult period. I needed to have a different kind of input about life and the difficulties of life, how to hold myself through my own anxiety and around the life experience of illness in members of my family. I didn't feel as though there was enough of that anywhere else. Maybe I just didn't find it in those places. It's not that it wasn't there. But I found it in Buddhism, in mindfulness, in the Dharma of Pema Chodron particularly, in the books she wrote – *When Things Fall Apart* for example. Because it felt that things were falling apart, the wisdom expressed in that book and CDs like *Getting Unstuck*.

And it helped to hold me through those experiences. And it did come through a whole different philosophical and spiritual standpoint I think, that I wasn't experiencing up until that point. And that still exists for me. I still go back and I still listen to Pema Chodron, and I still do some of the practices that came out of that period of time. In particular Self Compassion practices are important to practice as well as also learning to recognise my own egocentric stories as unhelpful. *Radical Acceptance* and *True Refuge* by Tara Brach stand out as important books.

Rosa and Katy also endorse the benefits of this approach, making it clear that this kind of practice is a whole person approach and not just a matter of stilling the `mind` in the conventional sense of the word.

Rosa: Well on some sort of fundamental level I think meditation is about letting the mud settle on a kind of psychic level. I mean I love the stillness, the silence. The mindfulness meditation has always been a way of stilling. As someone who finds the world outside quite a stressful difficult place in lots of ways, the meditation is way of being still and being quiet ... it's a restorative practice, a plugging in to the 'Source'.

Katy: So Buddhist meditation – vipassana – works really well for me as it's based on body awareness and is really very similar to the light-body exercise. Quiet contemplation, alone or in a group, is gentle, deep, and brings many gifts both spiritual and physical: relaxation, rest, calm awareness, better sleep etc.

Robert elucidates this view further, and also begins the process of mapping this kind of meditation back into Druidry.

Robert: Meditation looks into the mind to find its nature. The mind has two aspects, one known as the conceptual mind that sees everything as duality; the other is the nature of mind that is non-conceptual. The non-conceptual mind is the eternal state of presence that is a ceaseless flow pervading all things. The more we abide in that place, the greater our understanding of ourselves becomes. Meditation is the practice for knowing our eternal selves and an essential practice on any spiritual path.

Meditation practices as taught in the East immerse the practitioner deeply in the world of phenomena. They bring the world into a very clear focus. Meditation becomes a tool to understand the workings of the mind, to master the mind and tame it. Then we become aware of the conflicting emotions that cause harm and by being aware of these mind states we have the ability to observe them, dissipate them and leave us in a calm abiding place.

To access these states in Druidry, we must first enter myths that provide a container for this wisdom. Taliesin is a Buddha of the West and through his enlightenment we too can access ours. For though much of the old teaching has been lost, I believe these ancient wisdoms are here with us now, locked away in stone and tree, all we need to do is open ourselves to the wonder of nature and with dedication and commitment they can come flooding through.

Joanna is also concerned to embed her learning from Buddhism (in this case Zen) into Druidry.

Joanna: I learned about meditation while studying Zen Buddhism. I spent several years learning about and doing zazen – now popularly known under the secular term 'mindfulness meditation'. I still do zazen in my practice, alongside inner journeys, outer journeys and walking meditation. I meditate on Druid concepts and principles, and create my own different meditations based upon those ideas. I have a deep personal meditation that connects me with the land through the goddess, Brighde – the land upon which I live, expanding out to encompass all of the British Isles through the White Serpent – it's quite something! I meditate solo for the most part.

JJ and Karen introduce a slightly different note, since they have both been influenced by contemplative Christian currents and by Sufism as well as by Buddhism. Their bare attention contemplative practice itself includes a felt sense of the Divine. JJ also describes it as a "being place" that "seeds the day". For Rosa, influenced by both Buddhist and Christian elements, there is an additional therapeutic element.

JJ: I think I got the essence of meditation straight off. I think I was a natural meditator. However I wondered; so I've been on a journey that's taken me back to knowing what feels right, which is actually very simple and just being present: and yes - OK yes. Meditation for me is letting things drop and clearing the mind but it's also being present to whatever is and allowing space for it in stillness, for whatever needs to arise ... to arise, honouring what's there. It's like a fountain, more a flowing place.

In meditation I quietly come into myself, into my pure divine self, connected to the Cosmic Birther, or whatever you want to call it, that place within each of us which is divinity and that 'being' place - meditation is a 'being place'. I meditate daily. I do that, and thank heavens. That's a very important part of my practice - maybe not as long as I would ideally like to do, what with the other needs of the day ... it's usually 20 minutes or so, more or less that.

But doing it at all seeds the day, steers the day, takes me to a place alongside other Druid practice, or other practice, (often it doesn't have a name), which steers my course for the day, sets the intent. And my experience is that that becomes my reality. Steering my intent sets the course for my reality. And on that basis, yes – 'be careful what you wish for'. I know they say that. It's true. But it's a strange thing – and a key part of what Druidry has taught me: if I dare to wish for something, it can become reality – daring to set the intent, daring to point the wand or whatever, from the heart and from a place of integrity, that's become incredibly important for me, and I can't kid myself. And the Universe can't be kidded.

The key elements – and I set my course by them every day – are integrity, humility, grace and humour. And they are bounded by a mandala of beauty, truth, compassion and wisdom. Which are all bounded in turn by love. It's almost like, you know the three circles of Abred, Gwynvyd and Ceugant. Like them.

Karen: The word meditation is a semantic minefield! I used to be a purist and think that 'real' meditation was that practice of simply breathing, without object, into (or seeking!) the silent centre found in Zen, or true Christian contemplative prayer. I have tried many other forms. I do still find the Christian definitions of apophatic and kataphatic prayer useful. Mine is definitely the apophatic path – the via negativa, the way of Buddha. Now, however, I would probably *define* meditation as any practice that enables one to enter (or seek) pure receptivity.

Rosa: Well last year I started reading the works of Steiner because I was just interested to find out where was coming from. And through that - he's very keen on meditation - the other thread to it is the therapeutic one. Through therapy and meditation, both of them together are the tools for what Jung called individuation and that's been a very important part of my life. So Steiner's teaching is about trusting your own experience. His 'Foundation Stone meditation' which I use in my practice reminds me to reconnect to a place of source.

I did a brief guided journey last Friday at a workshop. And Pan in the forest said: "Your only task is to keep your heart clear". And that struck me really profoundly as that is what it is actually about. Meditation is a way of keeping my heart clear. And I was thinking about that last night. A clear heart is an open heart.

My tendency - particularly as I've got older my body's got painful and going out in the world has got difficult - is to close down. And that means the heart is closed, which is not healthy. So the meditative practice has become more important as a way of keeping my heart clear. And a clear heart is also an undefended heart and a place where I can be centred and alive. It isn't easy and I often don't achieve it. But it's like a kind of a check, in a way – 'is this something which is keeping my heart clear or is it something which is clouding it?'

Well that's a good way of looking at anything really, any activity, any thought, anything. If it's clearing then it's helpful. If it isn't then it isn't. So I guess that's fundamentally what meditation is about - clearing the heart.

In my own case a Buddhist influence coming mostly from Tibetan tradition has dissolved back into my Western Way practice (not Christian), but in a new and different way, so that neither of them is what it was to start with (see Appendix 4). It's also work in progress, an experimental space in which I try out new forms as insights and inner promptings arise.

James: My solo practice time is a period of about 90 minutes in the early morning. It begins the St. Patrick's prayer (aka cry of the deer) and the casting of a Druid circle – then moving on to a period of exercise and energy work, which themselves have a meditative aspect. These are drawn from a fusion of kundalini yoga and my OBOD light body training.

After a brief walking meditation, circling around my room, I sit, moving into an exercise in which I scan my energy body, physical body and five senses - aware of them, appreciating and celebrating them. Then I perform a stilling practice from the Western Way tradition. Through a form of chanting and successive shifts in awareness, I withdraw from involvement in time; I draw space from the seven directions to a still point at the centre; I cease all inner and outer movement apart from the breath – until all identity and awareness is in a single flame of being, withdrawing as if into the void, unbeing.

The return and renewal are step by step through a succession of 'I' statements, each of which I sit with for about 10 minutes. "I am the space inside the breath" expresses a primal re-awakening. "I am the stillness in this space" adds clarity and luminosity. "I stand in the heart of being" expresses an identity linked to source, emanating from source, distinct yet inseparable, in profound I-Thou relationship. "I stand as awareness" begins the full reintegration into 3-D reality. Awareness, once self-aware, wants to be aware of World, not only as witness but also as co-creative agent.

Daily Offices

The last form of meditation described in this chapter is the OSN Daily Offices, practised by Julie. The OSN is a monastic iteration of Druidry and its forms owe much to Christian, and especially Franciscan, monastic tradition. Meditation shades into contemplative prayer and Julie's form of practice includes working with prayer beads.

Julie: Meditation has a big role in my contemplative practice. There are the OSN Daily Offices four times a day which I would see as meditation as well as prayer. I see meditation usually as the silent following the breath type of practice and also visualisation. I do think that meditation can be seen in a wider sense; that of doing whatever you are doing in a meditative way and staying present to what you are engaged upon. This is something I try to work with a lot and I feel it could be seen in some ways as the 'prayer without ceasing' which is sometimes mentioned in Celtic spirituality and other traditions too.

My daily spiritual practice is done alone, although the other members of the OSN are doing the Offices too, so I do feel a connection with them. I have worked in groups in the past and continue to do that. I find both beneficial but I feel that the solitary practice is my 'foundation'.

Meditation helps to 'bring me back to centre', back into balance. It helps counter the many demands for attention the world throws at me, seemingly constantly. It gives me space to concentrate on my spiritual practice without feeling that I should be doing something else. I certainly find it calming and grounding, and it is a great help in keeping anxiety at bay. I am doing a study of dream work just now and meditation is very helpful with that as it is often during meditation that I will remember some snippet of a dream and then be able somehow to pull the rest of my dream up from my subconscious.

Meditation does play a very big role in my practice as a contemplative. I work quite often too with prayer beads. This really helps my meditation and prayer. I've developed a couple of sets of prayer beads in recent years which are very flexible and can be used with different prayers and chants. Stringing them is also a lovely meditative practice as long as you stay centred and present to your purpose.

Chapter 6: Being in Nature, Walking the Land

Satish Kumar (1) remembers: "For mother, walking was much more than a physical exercise, it was a meditation. Touching the earth, being connected to the soil and taking every step consciously and mindfully, was supremely conducive to contemplation. Our Lord Mahavir, the great prophet of the Jain tradition, attained enlightenment while walking. This was dynamic meditation. Mahavir was meditating on self and world simultaneously, whereas in sitting meditation one is much more likely to focus on the self alone."

This understanding finds resonance with many contributors. Nimue finds "taking people away from the world ... a bit counter-intuitive".

Nimue: So much other stuff seems to be about taking people away from the world. And that seems a bit counter-intuitive to me. I'm looking more to bringing people into more awareness of what's around them. And the active contemplation of physical objects, meditations that focus on the body, or that get people moving, and at various times I've experimented with all sorts of things.

Mark finds much of his contemplative time this way as well.

Mark: ...Or on a hill in the wind. So the wind batters me in the ears, large overcoats, lots of noise is drowned out. So meditation is quite a difficult process for me. When it works, that's when the light bulb moments have come. That's when that connection happens that you know is a connection.

I can't get there any more in the same way as you couldn't explain your connections to me. It's not something that verbalises very well. But that understanding of where you are in the 'Verse – and touching it, if you will, just making a contact, can happen during a good meditative period. And doesn't generally happen except through spontaneous 'oh look at that! Bang!' and you get that instant connection, which probably doesn't last all that long. But in a group or on your own at the right time you can drift into reverie and reverence and it's quite lovely.

I find walking is another way in which you can slip into a silent space. And I can slip into that even when I go walking with my wife, which we tend to do several times a week. There's a nice 3 mile run around the village up and over past the burial ground. It's a taxing walk because we do it at a reasonable speed. We don't necessarily spend the time talking. Each of us can drift into a silent space. And so it is another way of concentrating on the walk, concentrating on what's in front of our feet. And you start picking out that particular green on that particular tree or that flower over there, that bird singing on the tree down there, wondering if it will still be there. Those little things that take you out of yourself and all the other things that you should be thinking about. You know. Work today. Work tomorrow. How that went. What I need to do. So the natural world kind of takes you away from it all.

Julie formalises her being in nature, walking the land practice into a 'lectio divina' and shows that it can work in the heart of London.

Julie: I find it very enriching to be out in a natural landscape. That can be quite difficult to find here in the centre of London, but we do have some very lovely parks, nature reserves and commons. I find it deeply contemplative to just sit and simply 'be' in those places. I would see that as a communing with the spirits of place and with the creatures of the physical world who live there. Something I like to do is a variation on the practice lectio Divina. This is usually carried out in Christian contemplative practice using a sacred text; most often the Bible. As a Druid, I see Nature as my holy book and I use that instead. I pick up some small natural object and use the four stages of lectio with that. The first stage is just to simply be present with the object; the second stage is discursive thought; noticing and deliberately acknowledging the object and its features; whatever you notice about it. The third stage is prayer; how the object inspires you to consciously pray. And the fourth stage is moving into wordless contemplation. These stages can run in to each other and don't have to be completely separate, although it can be interesting to note which stages are more difficult and look at why that could be so, and how you could work on that area.

The technique can also be used with a landscape instead of some small natural object. I have found both very powerful from a contemplative point of view. Opening out one's peripheral vision whilst working in this way can be very helpful and also very calming.

I find walking the land very good for contemplation. Walking is done at a much slower pace than we often travel in cars, trains, and even on bikes, and you can see so much that would otherwise be missed. It brings, for me, a much closer connection with the land and with the spirits and energies of the land. Just walking, even in a city environment, can be very inspiring as you notice all those little plants making their homes in cracks in the pavements and crevices in the walls, and all the birds and little creatures who live beside us in urban environments. How resilient nature is! There are so many wild plants (which others may term 'weeds') inhabiting our urban landscapes, and so many beautiful birds and animals (which others may term 'pests') such as snails and butterflies and pigeons... so many. I always come back from a meditative walk feeling refreshed and more connected with all that is. While walking I bring to mind the idea of Druids having pentagrams marked into the soles of their shoes, blessing the land as they walk. I try to connect with this idea and feel the ground more consciously as I walk. This really does increase my feeling of groundedness.

Even below the city streets the land is alive and a sacred pilgrimage is possible when walking to urban sacred sites such as Parliament Hill and even Ludgate Hill.

This form of practice is also endorsed by Elaine, Tom and JJ.

Elaine: I think it brought me back to the insight I got from my experience in Cornwall. The insight I got at that time was profound, I became very aware of energy, energy in land and the energy in people. And that stayed with me. So although I've actively been using energy in certain other traditions, I think the idea of land and a relationship with it is very true in Druidry and I relate to that, but if I was to pick anything out, I do think walking the land – walking in itself and being out in some sort of nature and somewhere near trees – has always been important to me. Also the early morning practice of greeting the dawn, and also being present at the sunset, are both times of day where I like to enter a sort of contemplative state – I'd use contemplative there rather than meditation. I mean I'm not particularly a formal meditator.

Tom: I find walking to be a meditative thing to do. And just sitting on hillsides and the like. Time spent among trees. And I'm a member of a group of contemplative Druids. So that has become part of my life.

JJ: Sitting in nature, going and sitting by a tree. Being with trees, streams. It's a funny thing but in a way, you asking it makes me aware it's a thread which sits with me throughout, more unconsciously than conscious – in the sense that the natural world is more integrated and 'always with me' rather than separate and 'out there'. As part of my practice I try and touch the earth at least once each day – usually, early in the day. I've also been offering group healing rituals with and for the Land – both here and abroad – involving fully receiving, as well as fully giving, to the land.

Katy extends the effects of walking to canoeing.

Katy: For me, going for a walk is a very contemplative experience. Not a walk with a friend, which is an entirely different thing and excellent in its way, but not conducive to contemplation. Walking solo, on a route that is familiar, frees the mind to concentrate on what is around and allows it to slip into meditative mode, steeping itself in the whole experience of the land around. A steady walking pace provides a rhythmic focus, and the changing scene around – experienced by all senses or each in turn – is anchored by the steady walking pace.

Similarly, when I am out in my canoe I feel something of the same. Here it's a little easier to be distracted as I have to watch out for various hazards (other boats, fishing lines, odd currents and eddies etc.) But on a quiet stretch of flat-water like a scenic canal, the steady paddle-stroke provides the anchor and the landscape glides gently by, freeing the mind to sink into the experience.

David and Eve have a more extended view of this kind of practice. For David, there is an intent to commune with spirits of place. This is one of the "central 'pillars'" of his practice.

David: In my own practice, walking alone with a view to fostering communion with the nymphs (spirits of place) and regular Daily Offices of prayer are the central 'pillars' of my practice alongside meditation.

Eve would like the practice, especially in a group context, to be more "doing" – not just walking and being meditative, but "healing the earth", being "for nature" as well as in it – especially given the current planetary crisis.

Eve: I think the walking of the land is important to me, because – quite a few years – may be 15 years ago I decided that every day I would walk, and I'm lucky to live in a place where I can do that, and then I would chant, and then I would pray. So in a sense that became a very powerful tool and practice for me. And I'd like, somehow I'd like to see our group, doing that more. Not just walking and being meditative, but more focusing on healing the earth. We're in a crisis, the planet's in a crisis, I think that maybe potentially, our group - that could be something that we could develop together, potentially. A contemplative practice with a focus on healing. Reading Joanna Macey and Chris Johnstone's book *Active Hope* has influenced me. Locally to me one woman started a campaign *Wool Against Weapons* and it has snowballed - seven miles of knitting which will stretch from Aldermaston to Burghfield has been done and sewn together as a campaign against spending money on weapons. It has happened through one person hitting on something that many others could resonate with. It makes me wonder whether within contemplative practice there is a way of giving healing; turning our collective energy more towards specific healing of say insect pollinators, governments, war torn places, specific ways of resonating with each other and opening that out to heal the planet.

References

1: Kumar, Satish (2002) *You are therefore I am: a declaration of dependence* Dartington, Totnes, Devon: Green Books

Chapter 7: Group Practice, Life Practice

Working together

Chapter 7 took us out of solitary practice to the world outside us, walking the land. This chapter takes us out in a different way into group practice, where we connect with each other, and into life practice – living with awareness in the everyday. Most of the material about group practice is from the experience of the Druid contemplative group in Gloucestershire. Elaine, JJ and Karen talk about its value overall.

Elaine: I do like the Druid Contemplative group I'm in, this is where I sit with others in contemplation and drop into a more receptive mode of being. Working with a group often intensifies my experience of meditation. I'm enjoying the current group I'm with as it is exploring a receptive form of meditation together. Everyone's doing their meditation in different ways, however being sensitive to energy I find that experiencing the energy level of people who are also in a meditative state feels really good. It helps me deepen my own state and I find that very valuable. I mean I'm not particularly a formal meditator but I like to have the support of the group; that's when I will put aside the time to meditate, to actually sit quietly within a group and I feel that is valuable. It doesn't have to be any more for me. I like being within a group that practices sitting in silence and also some vocalisation and sharing at the end of it. That's very nourishing for me. It's a deep sharing. I would always like to have somewhere to do that.

JJ: I think meditating alone is very powerful. And there is a place for it, in my case a need for it - and it's like a deepening. But coming together, when two or more meditate, it kicks into... it's like a generator; it's like – well, what we experienced today - it's phenomenal really. When people come with like-mindedness, with common intent, from a place of total presence and total vulnerability and also authenticity and integrity, yes, coming prepared to be open but present and real, into stillness together, I don't know - each heart a spiral or beating pulse, I mean there's something quite beyond description – something wonderful can happen, often happens, and generally does happen. In stillness, in a group, sitting together with other people, I experience wholeness and Oneness and yet connectedness at the same time. It's like a generator of contagious love; we catch it from each other and amplify it somehow.

Karen: I've always been a solo meditator by preference, so I've been delighted to find our group a nurturing space in which to meditate, and the group itself seems to have none of the 'specialness' that has kept me out of groups in the past.

Katy and Tom name specific benefits that transfer into the rest of their lives.

Katy: Essentially I work solo but enjoy meditating in a group when I can find one, as long as they do simple meditation. Quiet contemplation, alone or in a group, is gentle, deep, and brings many gifts both spiritual and physical: relaxation, rest, calm awareness, better sleep etc.

Tom: Benefits for myself? – I've already been seeing them. In my work and in my life. In becoming less reactive, which I think is a good thing. And I think I would give the same answer for Druidry as a whole. In order to behave and live in a more leisured and considered way I think it's pretty much a necessity. And I may end up returning at some point to some of the practices that I used to use in the U.S. before I came over here. But I've just been terribly busy since!

Mark names the value to him of a group culture that in a sense reinforces contemplative norms within a wider life of doing.

Mark: I need to find a space where I can switch off everything. One of the huge benefits of the contemplative group is that it's so much easier to be silent and to still the mind when other people round you are silent and stilling their minds. You can't pause in your meditation when you're in silence. You can't say 'I'll just park that and do this. I can go back to that'. Because you can when you're on your own. I find that little ear worm coming in, tapping you on the shoulder and saying, 'do this and do that'. And you say 'OK' and do this just to shut you up and then go back to being silent. And you lose that connection. In a group it's impossible to be not silent. (Laughs). It wouldn't work well, would it? The group pressure works the other way. And in a group you're guided to a silent place that you can't achieve on your own.

Penny makes a wider point about collective stilling and quiet space, especially in relation to OBOD gatherings. She is particularly thinking of the kind of work that facilitates contact with the 'Inner Grove' of Druidry, through paying attention to the psychic and subtle realms – thereby bringing in another dimension of connection and relationship in our work.

Penny: I think for groups of people who are practising together, it's of huge value to have quiet time together, to allow the space for that. I'm reminded of Tudor Pole, who started the silent minute, after a message from a dead soldier from the First World War, who said "we would like to help in the war effort, you must make space for us". That work of all going to the same place in an inner visualisation is vitally important, like a bonding exercise, with each other and in the inner realms.

Contemplative creativity

A number of people find a contemplative creativity in other activities, particularly creative arts. Eve, Rosa, Tom and Julie emphasise this dimension.

Eve: I felt very held by the tutor in the second year, in the Ovate. I found her extremely useful, how she responded very specifically to my practice and to my experience. I found that very helpful. And at the end of the – about 8 years ago – at the end of doing the Ovate year you had to make something, and somehow what poured into me was working with textiles and embroidery and somehow something took off. So that led on to my spiritual path being poured into making something, and being creative enterprise. That was totally unexpected.

Rosa: All my life I've made things – figures and images and pictures that have been an expression of my inner journey. So it's a means of getting it out, letting it out, and it's an activity that I really love and that I feel completely myself, connected... it's really grounding in that sense. I am mostly pleased and satisfied to make objects and pictures that represent my inner life. I've recently made a picture of a chapel in a forest with an equal cross on the table and a blue stained glass window behind the cross with a blue light coming from the window into the chapel. The blue light outlines a figure who isn't there, in a meditative position. The figure is an empty space and there are windows on either side of the chapel with faces from the forest looking in. So it is surrounded by the forest and creatures of the forest and that is my inner landscape. A very, deeply ancient chapel in the forest with an empty space inside. And I feel that kind of encompasses all that I am, and more than words can. And so that's the value of my creative life and the things that I make. They express that something which I can't express in words.

Tom: Yes. Well it's certainly part of my work as I am a visual artist. That's integral to what I'm doing every day. It has to be. Otherwise I'd end up going through the motions, which is something not to be desired.

Julie: I think craft work can also be a very contemplative activity, particularly when using materials which would perhaps otherwise be thrown away, such as using left-over fabric to make rugs. That kind of work brings a contemplative experience for me too.

Karen talks about creative and dynamic, potentially ecstatic forms of spiritual practice, in ways that imply a special value in these practices when they are, in their moment, infused with stillness as well.

Karen: Examples would be: Sufi whirling; walking a drum rhythm in circle, with a particular simple step; walking in nature whilst breathing consciously and gazing without naming; musical chanting: either short mantra or simply the vowel sound 'aaaahh'. Though thinking about it as I write, I'm not sure whether they would be so useful to me without my foundation in silence.

Extending to the whole of life

JJ, Joanna and Robert are particularly clear in showing how a whole raft of practices can have a contemplative element as understood by this group. Indeed this element can extend into any aspect of life. Indeed a contemplative life is really working only when it does.

JJ: It's become a thread which resonates and permeates everything I do. I think – in fact that it's essential... that's why I do it. It permeates and infuses and enthuses all I do. It can take form anywhere. I think that I now carry it everywhere with me: I can be in a greenhouse working for example, that's easier maybe, but bringing it to places - more challenging places – for example working with these difficult teenage lads, 'ditch work' as I call it; the not-so-pleasant stuff. Trying to bring presence and a meditative quality to difficult situations. Though saying that, I often don't manage it, but I'm aware that it does permeate what I do when I'm at my best. So meditation – it's funny isn't it? – It's almost like 'from the passive to the active', it's from the passive – in one sense passive – but it's actually very active, and it's an active force in the world for me. It manifests as an active ... beauty. Coming out of, seemingly ... nothing.

Joanna: I think everything that we do can have a meditative or contemplative quality – from washing the dishes to walking down the stairs. If we really pay attention to what it is that we are doing, everything can take on a different quality – deeper, with real intention behind everything. I sometimes chant, I have my own dance company and so see dance as meditation as well as communication without words. Drawing is meditation for me. Playing an instrument. Writing. Making love. The possibilities are endless.

Robert: Chanting leads us towards a contemplative state, using the voice as a tool, as meditation uses the mind. Our body is a pathway to the divine and everything we do can be aligned to our spiritual path. Dancing and contemplative walking use the movements of the body. These are simple ways to express our devotion and approach the light that is Awen. All these practices are there to help us become Awen. Contemplation is present in all our life, eating a meal, making love, shopping, it all is infused with contemplative mind. Consciousness accords with the natural world flowing through us. Everything done in a contemplative state is a source of wisdom.

Creativity works with subtle energies and brings them into form. Through contemplative practice I can be free in the formless world and thus bring back images and words from the source, or 'soul of Druidry.' To connect in this way we need tools to access states of consciousness unused by many people. Druidry teaches guided path working, the light body exercises within OBOD and the rituals that celebrate and honour our connection to nature and the spirits that live there. I believe that we need an ongoing conversation with these entities and I have daily practices to engage with them, offering food, incense and prayers in a mindful way, these rituals are beautiful and profound. Done with contemplative mind they become a part of life, allowing time to consider other forms of sentient life, connecting me to nature and restoring the energies that flow between my body and the land.

Chapter 8: Awen

Awen is classically seen in Druidry as the power of inspiration, and in particular the creative force for poetry and prophecy. It is what transformed the boy Gwion – though not before further trials and transformations – into Taliesin, the radiant browed Bard. Many of the participants in this work uphold this tradition in its conventional form. Others seek to extend the traditional meaning better to express their own experiences and aspirations. Some don't connect with Awen experientially and treat it as a convention – mainly as a shared chant, which brings Druids together.

Traditional views

Tom and Penny – in slightly different ways – articulate a traditional view of Awen, anchored in a view of creative inspiration connected to Mystery (Tom's word) or the Divine (Penny's).

Tom: Before I discovered Druidry and met other Druids, I used the word Mystery. And I thought of myself as someone who served – that, when I was doing my work, which was most of the time. And then when I encountered Druidry, Awen seemed to be an even better word because it is as far as many people are concerned, tied to inspiration. And that is something I hold as central and dear. So yes, that large whatever it was that I encountered and experienced as a very young person I now describe as being in Awen.

Penny: I see Awen as an untranslatable experience; probably it's an untranslatable [Welsh] word, but the resonance of the 'wen' sound is to do with divinity and whiteness and lightness and so on.

A lot of people talk about Awen when they're talking about the flow of energy, and I think that's erroneous. I think it's to do with inspiration. And I equate it with the lightning bolt; that light bulb moment. That bang. When you've done loads of work on something, you go to sleep, and bang! You wake up and suddenly you've got the idea for a book or painting or whatever – like the inventor of the sewing machine. He had a dream of pecking birds and woke up knowing how the sewing machine mechanism could work. So Awen to me is that lightning stroke of inspiration. It makes things clear to you and it makes your next phase of creativity... progresses you along.

I use the word as the chant, because the job of Druids is to be creative beings; so we call to the Awen, the source of inspiration and I think it's also a very appropriate way to bless each other and the land when we are in a group together. That's how I see it being used. I always remember Philip Shallcrass talking once about hearing the Awen being sung and imagining this great cauldron tipping out its blessings upon us.

Now somewhere in the flow of Nwyfre, the life force, there are these jagged bolts of inspiring energy, which we cannot predict. And in fact that's one of the reasons for being contemplative, because if you don't make the time and space, how is the inspiration to come in? If you're so busy preparing for it, 'doing' all the time, you know, there is no free space.

I think the path of Druidry is a path of doing, particularly – I think it appeals to people who want to make their mark on the world, who want to develop themselves in the world to be responsible and of use in their community. But without the contemplative parts we would miss a very important part of that development.

Awen not 'internalised'

David, Katy and Rosa say that they don't have a real felt-sense of Awen, though for Rosa it does act as a trigger to bring her awareness into the sacred, as OM and Amen do in other traditions, and there is a possible link to healing through sound.

David: It is the mark of a valuable concept that it is capable of multiple interpretations! Emma Restall Orr understands Awen as 'flowing spirit', but that phrase doesn't convey much content to me. Rather, I find the classical definition as 'poetic inspiration' much easier to grasp. Overall, Awen isn't a concept I find myself dealing with much in my everyday practice.

Katy: Awen doesn't manifest in my contemplative practice, not in any conscious way. Like the Holy Spirit in Christianity, it's a mystery to me. I've never experienced anything I could understand to be Awen. I'm not sure what people mean when they speak of it.

Rosa: I don't think I've completely internalised Awen actually. To me it's more a word than a thing or a practice or an essence. And I love chanting it but it hasn't got any more connotations for me then OM or Amen. There are those three words... OM connects me to Buddhism and Amen connects me to Christianity and Awen connects me to Druidry. And they're all ways of kind of bringing my awareness into the sacred and they all feel very ancient. Sound is also really important I think.

I do another kind of practice, which is singing exercises. I do them most days, mainly to keep my voice clear but also sound is another very powerful way of bringing me into use a centred place.

Yesterday I was feeling quite scattered because my body was hurting and I just started doing the singing and it was a feeling like warm wind on my back, warm balm. It just filled me inside and outside. So I suppose in a sense this is part of that sound, the Awen, a resonating sound, resonating me to a certain state of awareness.

Modified views of Awen

Some people have modified views of Awen, which include a strong element of a traditional link with inspiration, whilst adding something new. Elaine talks about the vatic side of Awen as traditionally understood, but in relation to contemplative experience she extends her previous definition to include "the sense of Awen being present or the energetic nature of the world and being there with it, not separate from, not subject/object but being with it".

Eve talks about her own Bardic nature and Brighid as her personal source of inspiration, but adds experiences "that happen to me in nature like birds appearing synchronistically or flowers or butterflies or trees, or being with nature – that for me is Awen. It's being blest".

Mark has a "light bulb moment" view of Awen, but links it to a cosmology in which the "'Verse" seeks self-awareness in our moments of being Awenydd, and likens Awen to "the Holy Spirit moving through me". JJ understands Awen as "flowing spirit and the creative force" and Nimue experiences Awen "very physically as a flow and as a force – not all the time – and usually only if I'm deliberately looking for it".

Elaine: I particularly relate to the vatic kind of Awen experience and if I would call myself anything it wouldn't be Druid – I would like to call myself one of the Awenyddion if I only could get my Anglo Saxon tongue correctly around this Welsh word. Perhaps I can take the name of one of those inspired by the Awen. That is what I'm about.

Alternatively there might be the more active possession of Awen created by chanting the Awen or vibrating the word Awen. It is the activation of something and the reception of something. I'm letting something flow through, often poetry or words or even just being in touch with where my body is at the moment, becoming really being present.

Interestingly we had a seed group which was about exploring the Awen and now our contemplative Druid group also invokes Awen. I find that when we do this it creates a free flowing almost vatic flow, which is not just being quiet but also then giving voice. So I think it's just a shift from the silence into making a noise or a vibration. It is part of the same continuum.

I do like the term Awen, being in flow with the Awen and Awen being present. In contemplation I think it's just the sense of Awen being present or the energetic nature of the world and being there with it, not separate from, not subject/object but being with it.

Eve: I think it's just a question of putting the word to the experience, really. I think it's something about inspiration, it's being able to feel the inspiration and allowing the inspiration to flow, the creativity to flow. And that's quite hard. I'm quite a Bardic person in many ways and that's happened so much in the past on my own or in nature, but bringing it into a group – I enjoy what we do when we do that together, collectively. I think that there's more – I would like to have more opportunity to be with the group in nature, with that expression. I think that could be an important piece.

And I've put here, "Brighid is my inspiration". And sometimes, she is my connection to Awen. And specific things that happen to me in nature like birds appearing synchronistically or flowers or butterflies or trees, or being with nature – that for me is Awen. It's being blest. I often feel blest by an experience. I might be doing Qi Gong on a beach in Cornwall and suddenly a pod of dolphins comes by – you know, that kind of thing. So those sort of things are deeply important to me. And I think as our group develops we could perhaps manifest that together in some way. Especially on the day sessions.

Mark: Well that's that connection. That is kind of what you are trying to achieve. In every spiritual practice that's trying to make contact with their deity, god, pantheon, however else, there is that connection. And it's like a lightning bolt. It's like that Michelangelo thing, really, isn't it? When you touch that connection, then it is like that lightning bolt. And I do work in 400,000 volt sub-stations so I know what that looks like. *(Laughs)*. The Awen is expressed as that creative urge or connection with creativity and that follows for me neatly for me into the 'Verse. You know, the fractured everything – a part of me, a part of you, a part of this table. And on a level, making that connection is like everything connecting back up again. Just, I suppose, with a slightly engineering head on, if the singularity of the 'Verse fractures itself into an infinite number of things – the big bang if you will - positing, just so that it could look at itself in more detail – then everything out there is part deity. And if it all came back together again it would be deity reborn if you will. So, channelling that connection to the creative urge, the Awen if you like, is like trying to bring all these disparate fragmented parts of the universe back together again. And so it's a term that's used in Druid tradition and there are all sorts of things you know – 'I'm channelling the Awen so I can write my book'; 'I'm channelling that Awen so that I can visualise this painting' or I'm seeking connection to deity. It's analogous to the Holy Spirit that is moving through me.

JJ: OK. Awen as flowing spirit and as the creative force, and as that flowing – yes that spirit of wonderment, I was going to say, in one sense, in a funny sort of way, contemplation and Awen sit as bedfellows, but they also feed each other. Meditation for me is the place of silence and stillness. Awen is the place of potent outflowing and creative force. And the one comes from the other. They each come from the other in a funny sort of way. So there's some intertwining. Awen, for me, yes the spirit of flowering, as individuals as universe, as creative force. Something in there - and none of that! I perhaps tend to think of flowering unto thyself, but it's also intimately connected to the magic of the breath. So Awen could be called 'Breathing Magic'.

Nimue: I experience it very physically as a flow and as a force – not all the time – and usually only if I'm deliberately looking for it. But I tend to be deliberately looking for it if there's music or if there's public speaking or if I'm writing. So there are more days than not when there's an attempt to tap into that. But it is like a physical force. And it comes up through my feet. And I feel it very physically as a presence. It changes how I think and how I feel and to a certain degree even who I am, if I'm flowing with that and if I'm doing whatever it causes me to do. My consciousness of it as a sacred inspiration is something that is inherently spirit and that sometimes has its own intentions. And it can be incredibly powerful. It depends on what I'm doing with it and what it's doing with me, and when it's not there that's disturbing and disorienting and I get patches of that as well.

Innovative views of Awen

Julie, Joanna and I find most resonance in Awen as a name for connectedness. It is in this sense of Awen that Julie finds the contemplative aspect. In this sense Awen can be understood as "grace". Joanna connects with "flowing spirit", a term attributed to Emma Restall Orr, though she says that this usage can be "both helpful and confusing" and concluding that whereas Druids understand "Nwyfre" as the life force itself, "Awen" can be seen as that which connects us, the tool for "tapping in". I describe Awen as a "word of power" that connects modern Druids, and "in the poetry of practice", the primal breath and energy of the Cosmos. Druids working together can change our relationship and the space by working with Awen, since "we are gathered together in sacred space and time".

Julie: Yes, I do tend to feel Awen as being 'flowing spirit', but also as the energy which links us all together. I feel it does have an inspirational aspect to it as well as being a unifying energy. It is in this sense of Awen flowing through everything that I find the contemplative aspect. Perhaps Awen is also 'grace'; that which suddenly appears unbidden and unexpectedly.

Joanna: I think it was Emma Restall Orr who first defined Awen as 'flowing spirit' – before it had been called poetic inspiration, if I am remembering correctly. The idea of incorporating the word, 'spirit', into the description is both helpful and confusing: helpful, because it provides a sort of animistic view of everything, confusing in that the word can have so many other meanings. I agree with flowing spirit, seeing Awen as that which connects everything in one beautiful harmony, each individual singing their truth.

Sometimes the definition of Awen seems more to me like Nwyfre – which is the life force. Maybe Nwyfre is the life force, and Awen that which connects everything living thing to this life force, the tool for "tapping in" so to speak.

James: Awen is a word of power that connects modern Druids, as chant or mantra, especially when chanted by a group. In the poetry of practice, Awen resonates like the primal breath and energy of the Cosmos, a subtle pulse and vibration underlying the apparent world, welling from a paradoxically creative emptiness. Sounding and hearing Awen can change our experience of the space within and around us – to a greater or lesser extent - and our relationships within that space.

In a group where we choose to recognise the space as filled with Awen, our recognition connects us. We are gathered together in sacred space and time. That's why group practice is becoming increasingly important to me, after a lengthy period of mostly solo working. Simple, spacious methods work best. That's how Awen works for me.

Finally, Robert's view of Awen is shaped by his understanding of the Taliesin story as a journey to enlightenment, with Taliesin himself a Buddha of the West. The aim of the spiritual journey on this reading is to become Awen. For Awen is the enlightened state.

Robert: Awen is the light that abides within everything; it is consciousness, the alive principle of creation giving sentience to all things. To abide in the state of Awen is essentially my principal Druid practice, the goal of my meditation, supporting the aim of my life to be flowing and one with Awen.

Meditation is essential if you are to ever *become* Awen. Without meditation Awen stays as a concept and, inspirational as that concept might be, it is a part of the mind that is caught up within the flow of time. Awen is beyond time; it is the eternal place that was never born, the ceaseless flow of presence. A spiritual path is a vehicle to know ourselves. The deeper we go, the more profound our experience of the world becomes. We can no longer look at the landscape around us as an inert commodity to exploit. We see it as our own body. In this one simple act of recognition everything is transformed, becoming a thing of beauty to preserve for future generations.

Druidry is about waking up and seeing the world as it is. When we can stand with courage and speak with a true voice that to me is the essence of Awen. Abiding in the light of Awen we are filled with wisdom and creativity, it flows from us creating all manner of things, music, art, poetry, dance and the vivid joy of living. It supports the goodness of life and helps to remove our self-doubts. When we become Awen we are filled with love and compassion, generosity and forgiveness, these are healthy states of being and Awen is the greatest healer. Residing there we are the light and can help others caught in the darkness of the world. We become the soul of Druidry. Instead of treading a path we have become the path and must now also become teachers.

Implications of these different views for the development of contemplative practice will be discussed at the end of the book, in a section of 'Reflections and Conclusions'.

Part 3: Potential

Introduction

The two chapters in 'Potential' look at what contemplative practice can do for individuals and what it brings to Druidry as a movement.

For 'doers', entry into contemplative spaces provides an opportunity to slow down (and even to stop). This can enable creative re-charging, better overall alignment to the flow of experience, and relief from the energetic consequences of busy-ness. Such spaces support being and connecting in a different kind of way. Sustained contemplative practice can 'feed' outer work (such as prison chaplaincy), and provide a stable foundation for honouring nature more deeply, working on inner processes, and finding an open-hearted space to process the distractions and dramas of the world and thereby let them go. It can ameliorate the worst effects of ego-driven behaviour through enabling a return to the centre and a clear receptivity to the present.

For the community as a whole, a contemplative strand becomes a resource for living more wakefully at the collective level. Druidry is a path of nature and nature is everything including the inner workings of the mind. A mindful stance thereby enters into our concern for the land we stand on and for the Earth as a whole. For contemplation changes who we are and how we work, including the way we approach charged areas like ethics and politics. Contributors are in agreement that action and contemplation, celebration and stillness, the extroverted and introverted aspects of community life need to be held in balance. For many, there is the sense that the action-oriented, celebratory and extroverted side is currently dominant in Druidry and that the whole movement could benefit from a gentle rebalancing in the contemplative direction. Slow permeation is seen as the best policy, and the most congruent with the contemplative spirit.

Chapter 9: What Practice Can Do

Valuing Contemplative Practice

Some contributors make statements about the value to them of contemplative practice that point to its potential benefits for Druids (and others) more widely. Some focus on group practice and some on individual. Below, Nimue describes her journey in the Gloucestershire group: "the stopping and then just being and being open creates whole other possibilities that are just not there if you don't do it". For Eve, the Gloucestershire group is a way of bringing her Druid and Buddhist influences together. Rosa looks at contemplation as a route to greater self-awareness: "knowing yourself really deeply, both the good and the bad bits. Becoming more self-aware, at this time of the evolution of consciousness is very important". Julie describes her practice as a means of "feeding outer commitments such as my prison chaplaincy work". She looks to ways in which Druid contemplative practice could be strengthened.

Nimue: I've found that really important in the last year. Because it's about the stopping and what happens when there isn't the deliberate attempt to achieve something. And I can end up over-thinking and too busy. But you don't get the same sparks of creativity and ideas if you are pushing all the time. And the stopping and the just being and being open creates whole other possibilities that are just not there if you don't do it. In terms of individual creativity that can be really important, and the kind of relationships you have with people, if you slow down with them, I'm finding very interesting. That's something I want to work with. And stuff that's just not so directional and not so busy. I think we have a great need for that in the world at large. There's too much busy-ness and not enough good stuff and I think that contemplation can really do something to help re-balance that.

What you've set up with us has been a really powerful journey for me. I resisted it actually, when the group first started, and said, 'Ooh, I'm interested' and then I didn't show up at things. Some of that was lack of nerve, and some of it was lack of willingness to stop. And it was a long time before I actually owned that and dealt with it. That I was afraid of slowing down and of loss of momentum. The first whole day that we did felt so odd and so strange to stop because I'm not used to stopping. And the transformation over time to get to a point of thinking, 'actually yes, this is a really good thing, something I ought to be doing', has been quite a life-altering experience in terms of how I relate to myself and whole swathes of stuff that I'm doing. So I'm very glad that you're doing this. I think it's very powerful work. And I hope there will be more of it.

Eve: I am encouraging a more contemplative approach to life generally. This helps me to be healthier and I encourage others to do the same professionally. The contemplation group has helped me to bring two paths into one. And I think I'm still in the process of doing that. I think our work with contemplation and the group helps me to weave them together. I don't feel split between two different pathways anymore. I know my true essence is my love of nature and it finds a home in Druidry and is helped by Buddhism. There is no conflict and no fundamentalism either. Contemplation is a modus vivendi, a way of living and being.

Rosa: I think the contemplative practice at its best is a way of developing the inner life and enabling people - myself and other people - to become more sensitised and more authentic and I go back to Jung's individuation... so that people become more self-aware. I think is about being aware of yourself, knowing yourself really deeply, both the good and the bad bits. And that I think the contemplation and the kind of therapeutic aspect of Druidry, the Druid practica as we call them, are also a way of enabling individuals to become more self-aware, more conscious. Becoming more self-aware, at this time of the evolution of consciousness is very important.

I think it's easy to hide behind all the rituals and the theatricality of it, and not learn about yourself. So it's a way of becoming... more self-aware and more grounded in reality. I think it's a vital part of Druid practice, having this contemplation. I can't see how you could be a truly spiritual practitioner without that. It is what's not there in Christianity, and what's so good about Buddhism. The basic structure of Buddhism is the sitting.

Humankind has this capacity for denial and spitting, all the stuff that makes life a place where terrible things happen, the terrible things we do to one another, all because we don't own our own darkness and we project it out. And I do feel very strongly that spiritual practice if it's authentic has to be a way of enabling us to own our inner darkness and actually manage it in a constructive way.

Julie: For myself, I feel that 'outer' commitments such as my prison chaplaincy work are fed by my own personal spiritual practice, which is very contemplative. My solitary work is the foundation upon which other more 'outward focused' work stands. My solitary contemplative work is really the spring which feeds those other activities. Having said that, some sort of sharing with others who also value the contemplative way of working would be valuable, whether that is in the form of writings, on-line groups, groups actually meeting together from time to time, or even retreat type work. I think there are 'pointers' towards the idea of a contemplative approach to Druidry. My own Druidic contemplative practice grew out of some of the exercises in the OBOD Ovate Grade course (old version), so there is a place for this type of practice to be developed within existing Druid resources.

Penny values "allowing space" through contemplation, as a corrective for a "natural doer". At the same time she is alert to problems of imbalance in the other direction and the possibilities of mystical elitism. "Balance" is her watchword, with the balance being struck differently depending on a person's "mix of active and contemplative abilities".

Penny: I think that the challenge of my Druidry is that I'm a natural doer. To allow space I think is of inestimable value. So yes, the more I allow space for contemplation, the more easily I find myself in the flow of the world and my place in it. Having said that, I think people make artificial divisions. I meet people who are naturally insular and there seems to be a certain cachet attached to that: as if it's a `spiritual' way to be – and that's a popular misconception, encouraged by books and films. But when you're expressing your spirituality in the real world, then the only way to do it is in accordance with your own talents and strengths; there is no right or wrong, better or worse: we must all respect one another's decisions as to how to balance the active and passive.

So my particular challenge is to slow down, but if you're a natural contemplative, may be the challenge is to be a bit more out there in the world. Otherwise you're approaching the way of the mystic, which was explained to me once using the image of the Tree of Life. Think of us in the world the Divine Spirit above, the mystic goes on a path which is straight up, which is lovely for them. But we are all social animals and we all have a part to play in society and our responsibilities, which involves us in exploring the other paths of the tree as well; to gain and be enriched by experience. So actually, to balance the two, exploring relationships and helping other people, being fully active in the life whilst keeping a sense of the spiritual component is what Druidry's all about to me.

Because the Druid remit is for service. The Druids of old were always of service to their community. If we remove ourselves to embrace the contemplative side too deeply and ignore that community interaction, I think we are missing a very important part of Druidry. It's all a big balancing act isn't it, the spiritual, the mundane and, how within the spiritual you express it and what time you give to each part of it. It's a fascinating challenge and one that I absolutely adore. Great fun!

There is room for every expression of spirituality in modern Druidry. All the way from what you might almost call `ritual Am Dram' for the more outwardly expressive people to the quieter times where you might have silent meditation for an hour, and everything in between. And not only when deciding what's right for us, what works for ourselves. I do think these things become easier when you're with other people and so finding a group to do it with helps enormously.

For Robert, contemplative Druidry is an "ongoing practice which never finishes", precisely because it allows him to be "present in all the actions of my life... aware of my actions and how they impact on the world". For in his world view, influenced by Tibetan Bon Buddhism, contemplation and action are co-arising, with no ultimate distinction between formal practice and the rest of life.

Robert: I continue to develop my contemplative Druidry every day; it is an ongoing practice that never finishes. It inspires me to be strong, to hold myself up when I fall, it allows me to be humble when I feel pride and love when I feel anger. It reminds me to constantly be present in all the actions of my life.

I try and speak with an open heart, I try and act in a beneficial way towards the world around me and I try to observe my ever moving mind, that is my spiritual path, being aware of my actions and how they impact on the world. Life is an ever impermanent display of phenomena that we are caught up within for such a short time, we can either get distracted by the world, caught up in its never ending dramas and emotions or we can stand outside of it and observe it from a stable foundation.

Contemplation for me is at the heart of Druidry; it is the place that gives life and light to this beautiful spiritual path. They are one and the same; when we see a beautiful sunset, watch in wonder as a storm ignites the sky with fire lightning, all these things are contemplative. We stop for a moment and just observe, that is essentially what meditation is, to be able to watch the world with awareness. It sounds really simple until we get distracted and once more we fall from that place of grace into what we need for lunch, does my bum look big in these trousers, do people really like me, oh god I'm getting old, will I ever have enough money to be able to do some of the things I want to do? That is my contemplation, trying to live with full awareness of who I am and navigating the many emotions that life throws up as I move through each day.

Karen no longer meditates as a daily routine, because a certain stance towards life has been achieved, supported by an ability "to return to the centre, to be receptive and present".

Karen: I don't meditate daily any more as a routine. And, without it, I wouldn't be who I am. Indeed, I dread to think what I would have developed into without it, an ego-driven floundering miserable idiot – and probably one who did a very nice line in spiritual holier-than-thou!

Of course, it's not the practice per se, but the results of the practice that are of value. We've all met ego-driven holier-than-thou meditators too. Not that I am ego-free at all; and, the ability to see that in action, to ameliorate its worst effects, to return to centre, to be receptive and present are fundamental to my inner life, my relational life, and the work I do in the world. It's essential to my life as it is and how I look to develop it within the illusion of time and space. (Since I am part of that lila-maya!)

Later Life and Awareness of Death

Eve and Rosa think of the contemplative mode as having particular value in later life, with Eve continuing that thought so far as to suggest the Gloucestershire contemplative group might give thought to death, and the preparation for death.

Eve: Well. I'm quite sure that there are a lot of people like me that have had a lot of experience, and who are at the same point. I do think in some ways, though not completely, that contemplation is suited to those of pension age! - To be more contemplative, to slow down and appreciate and have gratitude for the simple but precious gifts that are all around us. I find myself contemplating bees and butterflies at this time of year and simply watching them pollinating the flowers and collecting nectar. If we don't slow down and watch and contemplate such things we won't understand their essence and importance at a time when they need our help! Of course this skill needs to be taught to children from a young age too!

Rosa: As I get older I can't imagine a satisfactory life without a spiritual practice of some kind. It's the most wonderful adventure and journey and as I get older and less out in the world, the journey of Druidry through contemplation through ritual and through the love of nature is such a profoundly rich wonderful experience that I am immensely grateful for it in my life. It is very hidden from the world out there but I think if we're going to survive as a species we've all got to develop some form of spiritual practice and honouring nature, and to really live out the ideals of Druidry - loving one another and loving nature and working on our own inner process. So I think that's most important thing in my life. I have always thought that.

Since my teens walking alone in the countryside has been my contemplative practice and my inspiration. A painful foot prevents this now. I have internalised so much of that experience and I live with such wonderful countryside all around, actually not walking in it is less painful than it might be, although I miss the wildness.

What we do with our wildness has been something I have pondered all my life. I think that wild energy is channelled into my practice now. Sitting still, being wild, that's contemplative Druidry!

Eve: I think the other thing would be something to do with preparation – you know how the Buddhists have got a huge amount of material about death and something about preparation for death, which I think contemplation is. Just recently I had a very powerful experience; it was a lucid dream. And it actually came out of me repeating a prayer, or fonn, "Wild Lord of the land and sea, Wild Lord of the sun and moon, Wild Lord of the beautiful stars" before I went to sleep and when I was asleep I was chanting it and then there was an amazing experience of surrender and an opening out and it felt like the God and Goddess were present and it was quite a wonderful experience of there being a gateway and at the same time a very human struggle being on the Earth. So I don't know. I'm not looking for the extraordinary experiences. I've been there and done that. So it's not that. It's more that I think in walking the land and in chanting, and being in contemplation together, we could do some preparatory work for death. And that is part of being alive.

Chapter 10: Benefits for the Community

Perceived benefits for Druid culture

Contributors are not concerned only for themselves or small groups in themselves. They talk also about ways in which the further development of a contemplative thread could favourably impact on Druid culture as a whole. Julie, as representative of a monastic Druid Order, makes a particularly strong statement.

Julie: There is a contemplative current in many religions and spiritual traditions and I feel that the contemplative current could certainly deepen peoples' understanding of Druidry. I feel it could extend and enrich an individual's understanding of Druidry and their particular journey within it.

I often seem to come across the idea that Paganism generally is an 'anything goes, do whatever you want' type of path (if anything so undefined could be called a 'path' at all), and I don't feel that that is quite right. It's true that Druidry isn't a religion or spirituality heavily hedged about with dogma, but it does have a certain integrity to it even if that is difficult to precisely define. It is in this area that I feel contemplation could be helpful in getting people to engage on a deeper level with their own experiences and with the natural world; helping people to more deeply explore both the world within and the world without.

I hope too that the Order of the Sacred Nemeton can grow in its work as a contemplative order. The level of commitment required does mean that it won't ever be a large group but perhaps at some stage we could develop something like a 'Friends' group for people interested in contemplative work who don't particularly feel called to a monastic way of life.

Contemplative work will probably not be an area many people want to explore and work with in detail, but it could be an area people might benefit from experiencing from time to time.

For Robert, contemplative practice is "essential for wellbeing and growth" and Druidry needs teachers who can "help those seeking find ways of meditating". He makes the point that "Druidry is nature, and nature is everything including the workings of the mind".

Robert: Meditation and Contemplation are essential for wellbeing and growth if you practice Druidry or not. The simple techniques of mindfulness have proven to be as effective as anti-depressants. Druidry is a path of nature and to know nature we must enter deeply into it, that is called contemplation. It is essential that Druidry has within it teachers who can help those seeking to find ways of meditating. We must connect to our deep inner core and the teachings of meditation help to do this. Find someone who has a good understanding of the practice and take teachings from them, apply those teachings rigorously and in time you will have experiences, this is the fruit. I love Druidry because Druidry is nature, and nature is everything including the workings of the mind.

For Mark, contemplative practice is an aid to living in a more "wakeful" way, which to him is a core value. But he doesn't want to be evangelical about the practice per se.

Mark: I'm sure many people would benefit if there was more of it about. And it would benefit me directly if there was more of it about. The practice of stillness is worthwhile for its own sake. We live a frantic, busy, chaotic ant hill of a life. Most of us are working so hard that we are barely aware that we are working too hard. I think that the practice of being still gives us a chance to think – Emma's word – more wakefully. With more awareness rather than acting impulsively, meeting immediate needs and if more people took the time to be quiet and consider their position, consider their own needs, then probably the world would be a better place. So, in terms of expanding contemplative Druidry, I can only think that it would be a worthy exercise because most people would feel better for it. But I'm not one for selling anything – snake oil, religion, or truth. I've never been one to sup from somebody else's cup so I'm certainly not going to proffer a cup to anybody else, happily. Because I've never once suggested to my Catholic wife that she'd like to examine Druidry - that would probably be a very short conversation.

A number of respondents take the view that there is an audience-in-waiting for contemplative practice in Druidry, who have some existing engagement, but are not fully served by the practices and events offered by what we can now call mainstream Druidry. JJ puts the case. Katy sees the Gloucestershire group as a means of meeting the need, whilst also wanting it to develop organically, at a cautious pace, rather than being rolled out as a kind of model.

JJ: What I recognise and know is that within OBOD for instance there are a lot of people who are let's say less extrovert. What this tends to feed and serve are those who are less inclined to be 'out there' – those who are solitary, but not solitary, wanting to come together in a very gentle way. We all need – there is a need throughout - just like reverence and mirth, there's a need for 'out there' and 'in there' and there's a time to be a little more boisterous shall we say, but there's a real need and time to be still and quiet.

I know that a lot of people have felt that wasn't being served quite as well as it might be. So a contemplative strand or stream – it's difficult to see how anyone could argue against it and say "I don't really want that". Anyone in Druidry would welcome, to my mind, would welcome this. And the key thing – what I think it's value and the real gold in a sense could be that, like meditation often these days comes from the East and with a Buddhist flavour, you know mindfulness and that whole strand, and great: but for me, in the way I manifest it and what I like about the Druid contemplative side is that it's of the Earth, of this land, of nature - it has a real resonance for people – far wider than anyone who might think of themselves a Druid. I call it, "back to the Western Way".

Katy: I would love to think a contemplative tradition such as we've begun to explore in our Stroud group could grow and form a strong thread within modern Druidry. I have long felt that we quiet contemplatives are not too well-served by OBOD (for example) where gatherings are generally quite loud, extrovert affairs. This is all very good-humoured and very rewarding for those who enjoy big noisy groups, but contemplation should be part of any mature spiritual tradition, and there is a place for group activities that are gentle, thoughtful, quiet and meditative. This should not be just a solo activity, though solo work will of course form the backbone of a contemplative practice.

Where is it going? Hard to say. I think it is important that the seed we have nurtured into a young plant should not be over-cultivated at this stage. Already I sense that people are wanting to hive off groups and start training others. I understand the wish to share our experience, but there is a real danger in things moving too fast and the strength of what we have being dispersed and becoming something less. Let's not start rushing to do something. A meditative approach is slow and steady, allowing the mind the space to develop. We do not need to make things happen. Our plant will mature and seed when the time is right.

I do not think any spiritual tradition is truly mature until it incorporates an element of meditation/contemplation. OBOD does comparatively well here – it provides us with the light-body exercise which is a real technique we can use and learn from, and it makes it one of the first things we learn. I wonder if this is why people miss the importance of it – in a rush to move on to the later 'mysteries', they see it as elementary and a simple first step. But elements are fundamental building blocks, and we should work with them every day. (Back to a discipline of meditation again... sigh...).

So it is essential that we continue to nurture this contemplative element within Druidry, gently and *slowly* coaxing it into a fuller, richer, lasting life. Too much grows too quickly and then collapses. This is worth waiting for. Not only will a contemplative current in Druidry constitute a spiritual base for those whose practice is naturally more inward-focused, it will widen and enrich the good foundation of meditation already existing in the tradition.

David and I make a more general point about the strengths which a contemplative current can add to a spiritual tradition.

David: All great spiritual traditions have had a contemplative/monastic expression, or expressions – usually somewhat looked down on by the mainstream, but always bringing a much needed aspect to the whole. I think that in our activistic, extrovert-focused society, any kind of contemplative 'offering' is of value alongside the mainstream and without acting as a judgment upon it.

James: My sense is that Western spirituality, reflecting Western culture as a whole, tends to be busy and active. This includes Druidry. Contemplation offers a leavening effect. Contemplative states - with their attendant openings to peace, joy, poignancy, insight, recognition, renewal, and so on - increasingly permeate the whole of experience, with formal practice and retreat supporting that permeation. Contemplation doesn't turn its face from the world, for in truth there is nowhere to turn. But it can change our experience within it, sometimes leading to new kinds of action, sometimes supporting a qualitative shift in familiar actions, including other community practices. It touches our lives and relationships, our stance in nature, our creativity and culture, and the way we approach charged areas like ethical and political life. My sense is that a spiritual movement like Druidry can only benefit.

Elaine and Eve both think that there is a ripeness for contemplative practice in the community, which the work of the Gloucestershire group and other initiatives may help to support.

Elaine: Druidry and other traditions I believe will offer more of this sort of practice. When I look around I see more people are getting interested in this and more people are talking about it. I'm sure this is actually generating something and it may be more people will turn to contemplative practice and create spaces where they can do it.

Eve: I think if it were more – like you writing this book for example and bringing it to the consciousness of OBOD for example or other Druids – that somehow something could be more honoured and acknowledged and maybe even structured – certainly brought out into the collective more. So, I do think that. I keep thinking that children need to learn this skill of contemplation. They are more and more involved with technology, how ever are they going to learn to just be in nature...?

Robert looks at the bigger political and socio-ecological picture and sees Druidry, strengthened by its contemplative disciplines, as a force for change on the world.

Robert: We are moving into a world where our resources are going to become scarce, our food production is being polluted and our governments fail to govern effectively because of corporate greed and power. We have to see Druidry as a force that can bring change, it might not change the world over night but it can change who we are, what we think and how we behave in the world. When we do this we then become role models and it's through our actions that others become inspired, this is the way things change. From grass roots level we can make a difference, we can inspire a new generation to see the world with new eyes, it's our children we need to educate, we have to show them that there are alternative ways of living that are more efficient for the greater good of humanity.

The current paradigm only supports a few people, the rest become part of a machine to keep the cogs of industry rolling for profit. If we are to move into a better world we have change the way we work, we have to bring control back into our communities. If Druidry stays as some fringe spiritual belief it will simmer in the background. People don't need to know what we believe, it's all through actions that we're ever judged. To sum up my Druid practice I find only a few words, unconditional forgiveness, kindness, compassion, generosity and tolerance, those for me are the bedrock of a good human soul and if practiced each day of our lives no matter what spiritual path we have chosen to take we will be a good human being.

Joanna values Druidry's willingness to innovate, to be a changing and evolving culture, letting the spirit flow.

Joanna: We must never become stagnant in our thoughts – one thing that nature is always reminding us of is that things are in constant change and flux. Druidry today is not the same as it was during our Celtic ancestors' time. We learn and use what we know from the ancestors, but apply it to modern times and modern life. It could very well be the reason why the ancient Druids did not write their wisdom down – it stops it from becoming fluid, from changing in accordance with the times. If Druidry is all about flowing spirit, then we must let that spirit flow.

Reflections and Conclusions

This final section is divided into four parts: learning from the chapters; teaching and learning, Awen; where I stand now.

Learning from the chapters

This book is a fruit of the contemplative exploration that I launched at Samhuinn 2011. My intent was to reach out to Druids with similar interests, not to invent a new genre of Druidry. I arranged the book in three main parts: people, practice, potential. I worked with 15 people, including me, resident in England and active in modern Druidry.

Within those parameters, we are a diverse group. Yet we also have much in common. As children, so our memories tell us, we were open to nature, imagination and in many cases non-ordinary experiences. All of these held Mystery. Growing up, we looked for ways in which our experiences and intimations could be validated and shared, and in many cases it took a long time to find them. In many ways this is a story of neo-Pagan sensibility and its growth since World War Two. Unsurprisingly, several people report involvements with varieties of Witchcraft and also the indigenous shamanism of other lands, as well as with Druidry itself.

These leanings are modified by the influence of other forms of spirituality, most notably Buddhist philosophy and meditation, Christian mysticism, and other Western Way paths with Gnostic and Hermetic traditions specifically mentioned. Such influences are significant for contemplative practice.

We all now practice Druidry and most of us express strong Druid identities. Most of us are active in at least one of three organisations – the Order of Bards, Ovates and Druids (OBOD), The Druid Network (TDN) or the Order of the Sacred Nemeton (OSN), Druidry's monastic Order. This means that our contemplative practice is fully interwoven with our Druid embrace of celebration and creativity, our commitment to personal and collective healing, and our traditions of honourable service to our land, ancestors, and descendants, extending out to the welfare of all beings on the planet and in the cosmos. Contemplation is not a luxury add-on. It is a way of resourcing ourselves to fulfil our intentions more awarely and compassionately and therefore also more effectively.

Our choices about specific contemplative practices reflect our Druid culture. The visualisations and pathworking encouraged by the OBOD distance learning course have held and nourished many of us. The OSN has consciously created a Druid and Pagan version of the Daily Offices inspired by Christian Franciscans. TDN members talk about contemplative time as a way of cultivating the 'wakeful' attitude advocated by Emma Restall Orr. The strongest external influence, manifested in slightly different ways by about half of us, is the assimilation of Buddhist-influenced mindfulness meditation into our Druidry.

But formal meditation is not our only kind of contemplative practice. Just being in nature and walking the land are major settings for contemplation. So are chanting, movement and methods that involve creative arts and crafts. So are the activities of daily life. In many ways the essence of our contemplation lies not in what we do, but the presence and awareness we bring to it.

The interviews do not show any hint of the world-rejecting and world-denying disposition linked to the history of contemplative traditions. Although Christianity, Gnosticism and Buddhism have all historically featured this kind of denial, it is not characteristic of the Christian, Gnostic and Buddhist influences on this group – and the Druidry into which these influences has been assimilated makes doubly sure of a different, world-friendly view. Working contemplatively takes us more deeply into the world, rather than out of it, and we want to enjoy the fruits of our practice by living the lives that we have. People in this exploration are committed to engagement with each other and the wider world. The Gloucestershire group's practice is partly interactive. It's not just about people sitting beside each other, though some of that is included. And in the wider world, group members are engaged in a whole range of community projects and political activities.

Thus far, contemplative Druidry seems to be meeting two kinds of need. 'Doers' want a place where they can slow down, put some space around the dramas of action, and disidentify from busy-ness and its relentless flow of feelings, thoughts and demands. For those committed to a more sustained practice, there is the alchemy of inner transformation. Meditative disciplines are at the core of the "alchemical magic" which Philip Carr-Gomm discusses in *DruidCraft: The Magic of Wicca and Druidry* (1). This inner alchemy births a new subjective centre of gravity, from self to Self in Jung's terms, for which the image of the divine child is often used. The predominant message from the contributors is that, if we take the trouble to turn inwards, and work a little, we can turn outwards again in a different way, acting on the world with clarity, love and power. Skilful retreat is a life-changing and world-changing resource.

For most contributors, contemplative practice nourishes openness of heart and clarity of mind. It can find a place in any movement in which these qualities are valued. Unsurprisingly, it has long been alive and thriving in Druidry. But for me and others, the intentional discussion of contemplative practice has not had the focus it deserves, and spaces for such practice under the Druid umbrella are less common than they might be. Druidry is a path of nature and nature is everything, including the inner workings of the mind. If this becomes more widely appreciated, we can gently generate a more conscious stance within Druidry as a movement, building on our common concern for the land we stand on and for the Earth as a whole.

At the same time, we sense that this work does not lend itself to strident evangelism. Contemplative practice cannot be successfully imposed. People have to be ripe for it. For a long period I was either cold to plain sitting meditation or unable to settle. It's been a later life flowering. I'm naturally calmer now and I've got more time. On the other hand in past times I was very open to visualisation and journeying work, particularly in workshops, which I don't do much now. Other people have their own stories. At least one contributor has stopped the practice of daily meditation because for her the attentional shift has adequately occurred, the lesson has been learned and its benefits are sufficiently manifest in daily life. Different doorways open different possibilities to different people at different times.

Overall I would say that Druidry stands to benefit from having a stronger, more visible contemplative strand and more widely available opportunities for contemplative practice. My personal view is that those of us who champion contemplation will be most effective through a cautiously experimental approach, acting with both confidence and patience to develop our work. Druidry works remarkably well without a consensus cosmology or doctrine. We seem to have the ability to combine spiritual depth with wide diversity in a spirit of good-natured tolerance and pragmatism. These qualities are there to work with in the contemplative domain.

Teaching and learning contemplative practice

There are two ways of learning contemplative practice, as far as I can see. One is formal, or semi-formal. We could develop our own meditation teachers, particularly for a form of mindfulness meditation assimilated to Druid culture and beliefs. The most obvious mechanism is structured residential retreats that offer teaching. Alternatives would be dedicated classes and workshops.

People could take their newly acquired skills and frameworks home and continue the practice by themselves. This might be backed up by more emphasis on this kind of work in future editions of the OBOD distance learning course, or resources prepared separately. In the OBOD context, this approach is an extension of existing practice with an additional repertoire. Other Druid organisations would have other possible points of continuity to consider. In the interviews, Mark uses the phrase, taken from Emma Restall Orr, "wakeful, purposeful connection". This intent could be well served by a mindfulness style of meditation. Julie, of the OSN, already includes breath meditation in her practice, and also has a view of "prayer without ceasing" as a way of life – another way of articulating much the same view.

In formal meditation teaching, there has to be an agreed rationale and curriculum, however sparse and skeletal, at least at the level of the individual course or retreat. The interviewees for the contemplative exploration have learned their mindfulness practice in Buddhist settings. But these aren't the only ones.

There is an increasingly well-known secular mindfulness movement. There are modern spiritual schools like Eckhart Tolle's *Power of Now* (2) and *Integral Life Practice* (3) inspired by the ideas of Ken Wilber. And there are other traditionally Eastern options, offered in Westernised and updated forms, like Sally Kempton's devotional and contemplative Tantra (4).

It is likely that some Druids are familiar with these approaches and might want them to be considered as models for Druid training. So there are decisions about programme content. These approaches are not all the same. And a truly Druid approach would be different again, if it is to be more than just a bolt-on of something else. Yet my sense is that a highly centralised decision-making processes would have disadvantages; offering coherence at the price of a standardised product and the risk of some community resentment. Not a great outcome for a contemplative project. The other option is to leave largely self-appointed teachers to offer competing wares. The price here is a level of incoherence in the teaching overall, and possible questions about quality control. All the same, I think it's the better option for Druids to live with, and more congruent with our culture.

The second, quite different approach to the development of a contemplative lens is completely informal. It depends on being in a group whilst practising, rather than being left to work solo. The Gloucestershire contemplative group has created a template (Appendix 2) for people to be together in ways that invite personal sharing, silent sitting, silent walking in a group, and entry into a space of sacred connection that we call the Awen space. People make their own meaning out of the experiences they have, and sometimes we discuss our meanings and generate ideas about other ways of working.

Two other Stroud based groups have some similar features. One is the Aurochs Grove led by Nimue Brown, which is built primarily around sharing time, while sitting or walking on a local hill, which is also the site of a Bronze Age barrow, overlooking the Severn Estuary. The other is Enchanting the Void, led by JJ Middleway, which is built around the group singing of chants accompanied by drums and other musical instruments – and, crucially, the silence in between.

All these groups work through immersion in a more-or-less structured (or unstructured) experience, with no training or guidance about what should be happening for people. People simply absorb a shared group culture which is contemplative in the first case, includes contemplative space in the second, and is devotional with a contemplative aspect in the third. In the contemplative group we talk more about our experiences than in the others, but there is no teaching either of practice or of view: indeed part of the work is to find a language for our experiences so that we can build on them. The overall approach allows for considerable diversity of experience and view in all three cases, with unity coming through shared activity.

One downside – if it is a downside - of this approach is that it is limited to people, place and time and doesn't visibly connect with or impact the wider community culture. Another is that the quality of experience within the groups has an unacknowledged dependency on the more formal trainings, and wider journeys, of the individual members in other settings.

Awen

My reflections on the meaning of Awen come out of my reflections about learning and teaching contemplative practice in Druidry. Chapter 8, on Awen, looked at different views of Awen among contributors, and in particular a tendency by some people to extend Awen to cover resourceful contemplative states as well as its more traditional associations with poetic and vatic inspiration. We've done this in the Gloucestershire contemplative group and it seems like a good inquiry – because we don't have a fixed view of it, and as a Druid group we do sing the Awen together and let it lead us into our contemplative space. It rings true in the context.

I also find Awen (as *aah* on the inbreath and *wen* on the outbreath) to be effective in mantra work. But then I'm not meditating on the meaning of the sound – other sounds would work as well - but rather following the sound to what Sally Kempton calls the Shakti of the mantra, the power of the mantra, its inner pulsation and grace. By contrast, there was a stage in my meditative practice (see Appendix 4) when I almost replaced the affirmation "I stand as Awareness" with "I stand as Awen". It rang false. I make a series of affirmations, over a half hour period or so, using key words in my native language: space, breath, stillness, stand, heart, being. Why end with Awen? Awareness rings truer to my experience. I own it. I stand as Awareness.

If we develop our contemplative tradition further, we may find ourselves talking about Awen and the status of the term more, and I think we need to be ready for that discussion. No one wants to deny the older meanings, universally accepted as far as I know until the old British Druid Order (BDO) website called Awen "the Holy Spirit of Druidry" in the mid-1990s. The question is how we deal with the newer ones, especially if they become part of the language in which certain forms of sitting meditation are taught. Again, it may best be left to natural evolution, at the cost of some disagreement and misunderstanding, until some kind of consensus emerges.

Where I stand now

My own 'rose' experience, with which I began the book, was a lightning flash moment. It was state altering at the time and had lasting effects. Yet many stories teach us that the lightning flash begins a process, rather than acting as a complete transformation in itself. Young Gwion drinks the three drops from the Cauldron and acquires its knowledge, yet still has a long road to travel before emerging as Taliesin, Radiant Brow. In Arthurian literature, Perceval is brought into the presence of the Grail on his first visit to the Grail castle, but he is very young and cannot deal with it. He fails to find his voice for the necessary question: "whom does the grail serve?" In other words, he has the experience but lacks a necessary confidence and in large part misses the meaning. It takes him many years of questing and disappointment before he reaches the Grail castle again, for a second chance. This time he succeeds and can become, to use a traditional mythopoeic language, a light bearer and so bring a power into the world. Our tradition teaches that whereas the lightning flash can come early, making sense and use of it is the work of a lifetime. That is the real work, and a potential for us all.

The rose experience came in two stages. The original moment in its grace and beauty, and the peace and joy it released over an extended time, were a classic 'peak experience'. But it was only when I wrote my verse about it several months later, and in no elevated state, that it became a *gnosis* and a point of reference for integration into my ongoing journey. The substance of this is in the last line, which emerged unbidden, insisting on its place:

> And I am the heart's core, mover of mountains.

For me this brought about a clearer realisation of what it means to enter, however fleetingly, into the identity of the rose. Sally Kempton describes "the world and ourselves as a tapestry woven of one single intelligent energy". And, although wary of over-explaining the numinous, I could readily understand the experience in itself as one of unitive awareness within that energy. The nine words that end the verse add an invitation to make a difference, to be an agent for moving mountains, and to do this from a heart-centred place.

> I am Rose. I am wild Rose.
>
> I am Rose at Midsummer.
>
> The river flows by me.
>
> Fragile, I shiver in the wind.
>
> And I am the heart's core, mover of mountains.

I feel rather than hear the fullness of the note, when I am able to hold this awareness. I do not experience myself as framed fully to hold such an awareness all the time. Far from it. But my practice makes it easier to re-establish and hold more clearly and more often - and then I'm a little less prone to lapses into sleepiness and forgetting, and the half-conscious performance of a lesser, contracted identity. My sense is that many people on spiritual paths face inner points of tension like this and find their own ways of dealing with them. My own major learning from this book is that other contributors find contemplative practices a valued support and a way of staying open to the 'more than', to our fuller being.

So at this stage of my life, I experience contemplative practice as my best available means, not so much of attaining anything, as of holding, awarely, a presence and a capacity that is already latently available. The practice is like watering a plant. The world gains because it is better all round to have plants that are healthy and vital than ones that are wilting and undernourished. How else can they give oxygen to the world?

References

1: Carr-Gomm, Philip (2103) *DruidCraft: the magic of Wicca and Druidry* Lewes: Oak Tree Press

2: Tolle, Eckhart (2000) *The power of now: a guide to spiritual enlightenment* Sydney, Australia: Hodder Headline

3: Wilber, Ken; Patten, Terry; Leonard, Adam: Morelli, Marco (2008) *Integral life practice: a 21st century blueprint for physical health, emotional balance, mental clarity and spiritual awakening* Boston, MA: Integral Books

4: Kempton, Sally (2011) *Meditation for the love of it: enjoying your own deepest experience* Boulder, CO: Sounds True

Appendix 1

Interview questions

What first drew you into spiritual life and practice, Druid or otherwise?

Is Druidry at present your whole focus, or does it sit beside other traditions? [Prompts] If the latter, can you (and would you want to) identify a point of 'unity in diversity'?

Say something about how Druidry came into the picture for you and the role it has played. [Prompts] What particularly stands out in terms of values, beliefs, practices, experiences, culture and/or community?

Say something about the role of meditation in your practice. [Prompts] What is your understanding of 'meditation'? What kind(s) of meditation do you practice? Do you work solo, in groups or both? What is the value of meditation in your life?

Say something about one or two other practices you see as contemplative or having a contemplative aspect. [Prompts] Examples might be chanting, dance, walking the land, communion with the spirit(s) of place, contemplative arts, and contemplation within ritual. What is the value of these practices in your life?

Awen is widely understood and experienced as 'flowing spirit' in Druidry. Do you share that understanding, or do you have a different one that you might like to talk about? How if at all does Awen manifest in the contemplative aspect of your Druidry?

How, if at all, could the further development of a contemplative current in Druidry nourish and inspire your own life and practice? Where do you see it going?

How could the contemplative current help to extend the possibilities and potentials of Druidry as a living and evolving tradition?

Is there anything else you would like to say before we end this interview?

Appendix 2

Druid contemplative day programme offered by Gloucestershire group

10 a.m.	Arrivals and refreshments
10.30 a.m.	Entry into sacred space
10.40 a.m.	Self-introductions and extended check-in
11.40 a.m.	Break
12.00	Silent meditation
12.30 p.m.	Shared lunch
1.50 p.m.	Outdoor walking meditation
3 p.m.	Break
3.25 p.m.	Entering Awen in silence – speaking from within that enlivened silence
4.05 p.m.	Check-out and reflections
4.25 p.m.	Exit from sacred space
4.30 p.m.	Close

Appendix 3

Druidic 12 Holy nights retreat offered by Julie Bond

I would like to mention a retreat-type programme I am developing for the period around the Winter Solstice. This period has been recognised by many as a time of special importance for contemplation. Astrologically, the Sun is nearest to the Earth at this time and this is seen as a metaphor for the closeness of this world with the Otherworlds. Although for us in the Northern hemisphere it is the time of greatest darkness, the proximity of the Sun to our planet does mean that the Earth is being swept with powerful solsticial radiations. This can be seen as Earth being closest to her source of light and continuance of life in actual spatial terms, and us, as inhabitants of Earth, being closest metaphorically to our source of light, knowledge and wisdom.

There are quite a few programmes available for working with the 'Twelve Holy Nights'; many of them are astrologically based and some use Christian imagery. Because of this many of the programmes begin on December 24th or 25th. For this Druid version of the programme I begin it at the Winter Solstice, and it runs through 12 or 14 Holy Nights, each focusing on a tree in the Ogham. I use the liturgical calendar developed for the Order of the Sacred Nemeton (OSN) which uses a lunar calendar of twelve months plus an extra month every two and a half years. The 'extra' months are shown in brackets in the following list:

Birch, Rowan, Ash, Alder, Willow, Hawthorn, (Apple), Oak, Holly, Hazel, Bramble, Ivy, Reed, (Elder).

The idea is to work with one tree each day in the above order. You could use all the trees, including Apple and Elder, or just include the trees for the year ahead (or for the year just passed if you are using the retreat as a review). The retreat could be used either as a time of focusing on the year to come, or as a review of the year just passed.

For each tree there are Main Themes, Phrases, and Questions in the order in which the trees appear in the calendar/Ogham. As much or as little of these can be used as you wish. The idea is to work with the material contemplatively in any way that feels right for you.

You could work with a set of Ogham cards to have something visual to work with too. I may try to produce some cards/photographs of the relevant trees at the times of the year they represent at some time in the future.

Druidic 12 Holy Nights retreat

Themes, Phrases, and Questions

Birch

Main Themes: Beginnings; Cleansing

Phrases: A bright beginning blesses the endeavour; the blessing of beginnings - sparks light in the darkness.

Questions: What endeavours are you beginning?

Rowan

Main Themes: Protection; Magic

Phrases: A pentagram protects me as I proceed on my path; inspiration and creativity flow.

Questions: Which five protections do you have?

Ash

Main Themes: Deep-rootedness; Wisdom

Phrases: The key to wisdom deep-rooted in Earth; all things and all beings are one.

Questions: Where do your deepest roots lie?

Alder

Main Themes: Protection; Building bridges; Strong foundations.

Phrases: Oracular and protective, a shield for the heart; the healing waters flow ever onwards.

Questions: What does your heart need protection from?

Willow

Main Themes: Water; the Moon; Flexibility; Tides.

Phrases: Willow the Word of the watery ways; the Moon guides your waves and your whirling.

Questions: Can you be flexible when the tides change?

Hawthorn

Main Themes: Faery; Magic; Challenge; the Otherworlds; Fertility.

Phrases: Fragrant and fertile, the May blossom transports us; in magic the Otherworld brings union.

Questions: What polarities within you need to meet?

Apple

Main Themes: Avalon; The choice of beauty; The Otherworlds.

Phrases: At the peak of the wave my view-points are clear; all challenges ahead bring beauty. At the core of the apple lies the five-pointed star; an Otherworldly map of my soul.

Questions: Do the Otherworlds feel close?

Oak

Main Themes: Strength; Doorway.

Phrases: A doorway to the mysteries stands in my path with the strength I need to walk through it.

Questions: Do you see any significant doorways approaching?

Holly

Main Themes: Best in the Fight; Energy.

Phrases: Close-grained and dense the way ahead seems, I walk with directness and justice.

Questions: What are your main survival needs?

Hazel

Main Themes: Water; Wells; and Wisdom.

Phrases: Great well of wisdom, I sit within you in contemplative silence.

Questions: What are your sources of wisdom?

Bramble

Main Themes: Intoxication; Prophecy.

Phrases: I look to the future, my springboard the past. In prophecy I touch the Divine.

Questions: How do the Gods speak through you?

CONTEMPLATIVE DRUIDRY

Ivy

Main Themes: Spiral of the Self.

Phrases: I hold to my journey, my journey sustains me. My path spirals ever onwards.

Questions: Which turn of the spiral are you at now?

Reed

Main Themes: Transition; Directedness.

Phrases: (If there is no 'Elder' month to follow) At this liminal time I stand at this place. I go forth and a new cycle begins.

(If there is an 'Elder' month to follow) The gate is in sight, the transition draws near. I contemplate this liminal time.

Questions; What fresh inspiration does the world bring to you now?

Elder

Main Themes: Transition; The end in the beginning, the beginning in the end.

Phrases: The ancient wisdom is ever new; its newness contacts eternity.

Questions: What is ending, or needs to end, for you at this time? Can you feel new energies beginning to stir, even if the direction is still unclear?

The material above may seem quite brief and sparse but I have wanted to give plenty of room for people to work with the material in whatever way feels right for them. There are two meditations/visualisations which go with each of the trees (one for the beginning and one for the end; you could do one in the morning and one in the evening for each day) which could be used during the retreat. I am mindful however that this period of the year is often a very busy one when not everyone will have a lot of time available to spend on retreat work and yet they may want to have some sacred/contemplative focus at this time. I will probably develop the retreat material further as I work with it through the years but I would like the programme to be accessible to everyone who would like to work with it.

Appendix 4

Morning Practice Framework offered by James Nichol

My formal solo practice is based on one long morning session. I usually begin in the period 5 - 5.30 a.m. including journaling, this practice takes about 90 minutes. Although its keynote is one of space and silence, it is held within a Druid circle and a liturgy which continues to evolve with the experience of the practice itself – in a sense, gathering its insights and incorporating them in its structure.

In the East, facing East, I ring my bells and say: I arise today through the strength of heaven, light of sun, radiance of moon, splendour of fire, speed of lightning, swiftness of wind, depth of sea, stability of earth and firmness of rock.

Facing into the Centre, I say: May there be peace in the 7 directions; may the spirits of place flourish here; may I be present in this space. *Moving sunwise around the circle and I say:* I cast this circle in the Sacred Grove of Druids.

I again walk around the circle sunwise, starting East and saying as I move round: I thank the source for land (North), life (East), light (South) and love (West). May they continue to nourish me. May I continue to honour them. May the harmony of this circle and of my life be complete.

Within the circle, I do a set of 'rejuvenation exercises' (from a fusion repertoire of Kundalini Yoga and Chinese energy arts). Then, facing South I say: the illumination of lights, the illumination of the elements, the illumination of seasons, the illumination of days and nights. May light be kindled in the hearts of all. May my light be held within the greater light. Awen.

I take 5 'longevity breaths' (from a Chinese energy arts tradition) and then I move into a standing form of OBOD Druid light body practice, adjusted to incorporate elements of Kundalini Yoga. During and at the end of the practice I say: I am a child of the cosmos; the energies of the cosmos stream through me – I can feel them now, *adding on completion:* In the luminous heart of being, I am. *I begin a brief walking meditation around the room.*

I sit for meditation, the light body my subjective centre of gravity. Then I perform a stilling practice, based around the chant of OAI – *in a sense, backing into source and origin, and the edge of the void beyond.*

O: *(pronounced oh, hands in a diamond mudra over lower belly) stilling time, withdrawing from involvement in time... becoming time free... then timeless.*

A: *(pronounced ah, arms crossed over my heart centre) drawing space from the directions to the Centre, releasing involvement in space; resting in a simple point of being within.*

*I: (pronounced **eee**, hands together at prayer position over brow) ceasing all inner and outer movement apart from the breath, with 'I' as the moving flame of being, gradually stilling and diminishing to vanishing point.*

At the end of the chant the flame is at the brink of the void, latency, unbeing. I hold this point, before moving slowly and step by step out again, with the successive declarations, meditating on the resonance of each in turn for a few minutes: I am the space inside the breath; I am the stillness in this space; I stand in the heart of being; I stand as Awareness.

I embrace 3-D reality by scanning my physical body and senses, appreciating and celebrating them, moving on to feelings, thoughts and images, and from there identifying and working with intentions.

On completion of the meditation I say: In the luminous heart of being, I am. In the stillness of this space, I become. In the cosmic web of creation, I belong. Awen. A blessing on my life. May I be free from harm; may I be happy; may I live with ease – repeating the sequence for my partner's life, the lives of our kin, the lives of our companions, all lives I touch and am touched by and all beings throughout the cosmos. A blessing on our lives *(arms raised);* a blessing on the work *(hands over heart);* a blessing on the land *(raising and kissing my anchor stone).*

I stand, move to the East of my space and say, moving round the circle counter-sunwise I uncast this circle in the Sacred Grove of Druids, *and facing into the circle:* may the 7 directions be thanked for their blessings. May the spirits of place flourish here. May this work empower/inspire my life.

Turning and facing East I say: I stand today in the strength of heaven, light of sun, radiance of moon, splendour of fire, speed of lightning, swiftness of wind, depth of sea, stability of earth and firmness of rock. I ring my bells. *Then I make notes in my journal.*

Appendix 5

Aspiration prayer to Taliesin offered by Robert Kyle

Oh wondrous and awakened child who is ablaze with the rainbow brow

I aspire to you each day through my humble devotion to you

You who have known all times past present and future

I aspire to you each day through my humble devotion to you

You who have awakened to the wisdom of knowing

You who have awakened to the wisdom of truth

You who have awakened to the wisdom of awareness

I aspire to you each day through my humble devotion to you

You who have travelled through the elements and successfully liberated from them

I aspire to you each day through my humble devotion to you

You who have travelled to the farthest point in the universe and knows there is no where to travel

You who have been devoured by the goddess only to be birthed through her

You who are the path to her wisdom

You who are the light in the dark

You who have the illuminated mind of the awakened ones
I aspire to you each day through my humble devotion to you

Cherished one who knows all manner of things
Who knows all secrets and knows there are no secrets
Who is the knower and the unknown
You who have become the rainbow upon which consciousness dances
I aspire to you each day through my humble devotion to you

Grant me your wisdom to know myself
Grant me the power to awake to your voice
I am Taliesin, but to know you means I lose you
There is no self in you
There is no knower to know you
You are the sublime secret that stays silent on knowing
You are the one who is free from both birth and death
For you are the eternal child of the rainbow brow

I aspire to you each day through my humble devotion to you

Daily Practice

Druid Prayer for aspiring to be of service to others

I bend like a reed in the wind

I flow like water around stone

I burn with a passion to know my nature

I start my day steadfast on the earth

Each day I am born anew, like the sun may I shine with an eternal light

Like the moon may I come to know my inner being

I am a child of nature, born free upon this earth

May all my efforts be not just for myself, but so I might share with others the innate wisdom of knowing

Next a 5 minute silent meditation

Aspiration prayer to Taliesin

Taliesin, you who have awoken to the nature of knowing

Be my guide and master

Taliesin, you who have seen all times of past, present and future

Be my guide and master

Taliesin, you who have conquered all hopes and fears

Be my guide and master

Taliesin, you who have come to know the Awen

Be my guide and master

Next a 5 minute Silent Mediation

Prayer to the protectors

I call into the direction of the East; protectors of the earth please bring peace and happiness to my life and all sentient beings

I call into the directions of the North; protectors of the earth please bring peace and happiness to my life and all sentient beings

I call to the direction of the West; protectors of the earth please bring peace and happiness to my life and all sentient beings

I call to the directions of the South; protectors of the earth please bring peace and happiness to my life and all sentient beings

Next a 5 Minute meditation

Dedication prayer for all life

I dedicate my daily practice to the awakening of all sentient beings

May I by engaging in these virtuous deeds help me find peace within

Help me find the ever-present light of Awen

May it forever shine in my heart so it might illuminate the path of others

AWEN! AWEN! AWEN! Sing three times

Appendix 6

Facebook perspectives: Contemplation and Mysticism

Emma Restall Orr: How do folk distinguish between the path of a mystic and that of a contemplative?

Reg Amor: For me the mystical path is the seeking of and experiencing of 'spirit'. It's a deliberate act of searching for and engaging with 'spirit' and all its shapes and forms. Contemplation on the other hand would be considering or deeply thinking about the things I have discovered during my journey on the mystical path. This contemplation can often take years to come to any kind of enlightenment (if at all) after the mystical event takes place. If the paths had to be separated I would choose the mystical path, as experience of the 'divine' far outweighs the benefits of purely thinking about 'divine'. But what do I know?

JJ Middleway: The mystic contemplates Everything in Nothingness. The contemplative is mystified by the nothingness in Everything. Whilst the contemplative naturally accesses Divinity, divinity naturally accesses the Mystic.

William Brochfael Rathouse: How do you define the two Emma?

Emma Restall Orr: I've been sitting in the rain, splattered with mud, singing to the spirits, allowing the question to move through me. I feel the mystical path is more active, pushing the soul, adventuring, while the contemplative path is more that of experiencing the context of being. In this way, I relate to JJs definition above. I asked because I was wondering how others language the difference.

James Nichol: For me, mysticism is a stance towards life and being, and so a fuller word than contemplative; 'contemplative' looks towards a set of practices, or meditative ways of doing any activity – creative arts, peeling potatoes, reading, watching a wave or the sky. So in my use of words, mysticism would include both the things Emma talks about as mystical & the contemplative side as well.

Nimue Brown: I wouldn't claim to be a mystic, that sounds far too grand for where I am, but contemplation is something I do, and that feels a lot more comfortable as a word. I think we all tend to use the language that resonates with us, the reasons will be many, and seldom to do with clear distinctions of meaning I suspect. The doing is more important than what we call it. And I'm wary of trying to divide things up too neatly.

Cat Treadwell: Can you be one without the other?

Stewart Moonhare Talmage: I do not think you can, Cat. For me they are inextricably linked.

William Brochfael Rathouse: I like the concept and language of 'languaging the difference'. Precision in encapsulating concepts in words is undervalued by too many people thus we find ourselves talking at cross purposes. I hope you don't mind my nabbing that expression in my work.

Karen Webb: I'm with JJ and Emma. Re one without the other, I think one can though I wouldn't have called myself Mystic when I had my first full-blown experience of 'Divinity naturally accessing me' aged 12, I certainly wasn't a Contemplative. Since then I have learned to use Contemplation as a method, a tool to deepen my experience of Mysticism.

Nico Vermaas: I wish I could think of something, but after JJ's response that seems rather pointless ☺

Beer Schipper: I'm still contemplating about this subject ☺

JJ Middleway: a couple of related thoughts based on my own experience. Mysticism found me. It was a state of grace I experienced having been conferred from ...

... that will teach me, lost most of the message because sent from mobile: 1] keep it brief 2] quit while the going is good ☺

... Key points were: Mystic; a state of grace conferred from 'elsewhere'. Not so much chosen as 'it chooses you'. All pervasive and constant.

Karen Webb: Yes – a state of grace that finds you. Then, even though you know you can't hang on or replicate, you do know you can get yourself closer. And yes JJ all pervasive – even when I'm completely off-line and sunken in material seeming-necessity – always there. The reality of what is. And! Neither the mysticism nor contemplation have much to do with any particular deity. Though in contemplation a sense of deity may be useful, mysticism opens the door to not-knowing and the glorious beauty of the void – the nothingness containing everything.

JJ Middleway: Contemplative: A state of grace accessed through practice. Can become more and more a part of life to the point that one perhaps enters (or re-enters) mysticism. More a choice than something conferred or gifted. However the mystic can occur spontaneously Speaking as an ex mystic (I didn't seem to have a choice in the matter yet experienced it for several months), contemplation now 'points the way' for me. However I need to be more active in this, whereas mysticism was experienced spontaneously. PS final observation, JJ crap with modern technology:-J You'd noticed? :-J

Karen Webb: Yeah, noticed, JJ May be the same with mysticism, cos you say 'it was'. I use the contemplative way *because* I AM a mystic. As are you. Like vampires, once the Divine bites you there is no turning back. I am a mystic, I use contemplative practice to help me get closer to the emptiness that the Divine might enter. Whether that's valid or not I have no way of knowing, but it does help me a lot in daily life – much less reactive, for example! And She does visit gently from time to time. And, I know. When you've been taken by whatever-you-call-her, there is no denying. No matter how many people talk about brain chemistry.

JJ Middleway: Yes it's an experiential thing that changes the whole chemistry of one's being, such that "to know, know, know her, is to love, love, love her". Thanks for the observation that it's not just skills in modern technology I'm lacking: -J

Karen Webb: Reg, the first poster here, is right too because as the Sufi mystics tell us it's a search, a never-ending search for the longed for Beloved – spirit. Thank you Reg.

JJ Middleway: Another important point for me in all this, is that a crucial 'balancing component' is the resulting 'action in the world' (even when that is inaction!) because the result of contemplation is to 'remind and refine' the living of love in the world. Whilst the contemplative continually reminds herself of this, the mystic doesn't have that luxury because the mystic simply 'lives love' inevitably and inexhaustibly, as a consequence of being. "To Love To Serve and Remember" Where the contemplative and the mystic marriage courtesy of Rumi – who else?

"The heart is your student, for love is the only way we learn. Night has no choice but to grab the daylight; it's as if I see your face everywhere I turn. It's as if love's radiant oil never stops searching for a lamp in which to burn."

Reg Amor: Thank you Karen. When 'She' visits does she literally bring you to your knees? Do you become 'swallowed up' in 'Her' embrace? Do you spend days, weeks, months and years wondering what that was all about?

Karen Webb: Yes, Reg. Sometimes it brings me to my knees, and sometimes the human 'sensing' of the experience of literal ec-stasy, occasionally (rarely) of agony. I am 'taken' and the felt traces (rather than just the memory) may linger for weeks or months. I s'pose actually never left, after that first time. For me, though, I never 'wondered what that was all about'. Somehow I was graced with knowing just who/what it was that had taken me. All I knew, and know, afterwards is gratitude so deep it breaks that word and my heart wide apart. And so, like Rumi (thanks JJ) and all the other mystics I know there is nothing worth doing in life except pursuing and beseeching the Beloved. And, being human, again and again I forget that fact, become caught up in the world. And mostly She visits tenderly, kindly, reminding me in a breath so soft I could miss it if I weren't listening. I probably missed it a squillion moments – how many unlistening seconds have I been alive? And that's where contemplative practice comes in.

Reg Amor: Perfect! Just perfect! You have captured in a few paragraphs, that which I've been trying to express for so very long. Thank you Karen.

Andrew Jones: Nothing more to add really to what has been said – LOVE LOVE LOVE what Karen wrote! For me to put a language on it I wonder if contemplative describes my activity of reaching out to Her and mysticism is the grace of receiving the sweet embrace from Her?

Dawn N Jodie Diaz-Ruiz: Andrew, I like that thought a lot. For me, it resonates with my idea that prayer is talking to the gods (however one perceives Divinity) and that meditation is listening to them. It's like two sides of a conversation.

Karen Webb: Thanks Reg, Andrew, Dawn. I like that. And ... going back to Emma's post, somehow mysticism, whilst utterly receptive is also the more adventurous (there's always paradox in spiritual truth! Always ...). Willingness, thought-free, to welcome the embrace, to embrace the embrace, wherever it takes me... it occurs to me in saying that that mystical is also in itself both sides of the conversation (etymology to keep company with). Whereas in contemplative practice, and in prayer, somehow 'I' am the bigger part of the conversation? I'm directing even if I'm doing my best to listen too ...?

JJ, wanted to say how important it is that you talk about action and especially that includes (or maybe 'is'?) nonaction. The Taoist concept of wu-wei. Love does not impose or 'do good works' – yet always knows what the needed next action is. Such simple beauty. We do not need to escape from our dualistic world, simply to deepen our connection and respond.

Reg Amor: 'Willingness, thought-free, to welcome the embrace' but here are my preconditions! Don't embrace me with anything that might rock my boat too much'! How many of us to this? How many 'fear' not being in control in some way? How much 'blessing' to we fail to experience because of our timidity?

Karen Webb: Yup. And then there's that lovely Sufi story about the Seeker, who finally found the door to God's house. Just about to knock on the door, he had a thought, took off his shoes ... And tiptoed away ... and now he's free to happily carry on seeking, seeking all his life. Thanks everyone. She is whispering in my ear through your voices, and I am grateful, grateful.

Reg Amor: Mine too. Thank you folks.

Karen Webb: Fear... almost entirely a product of thought; yet the element of mind is Air ... And the other preconditions. "Prove you're worthy – do something for me first! Be on my side like the God of old." Or "But I need to be loved, it's so impersonal ... " Anger/pride and longing – so much more comfortable to hold onto, than to risk being free... oh, and that other one, it might all be a con. Chuckle!

Reg Amor: A con, is easiest to dispel. The 'whisperings' are very real as the 'visions'. Unless of course, the plot has finally been lost! But yes, a security blanket, because we are not prepared to let go and be really free. Because that would be really dangerous wouldn't it? My Lady has never asked me to give up this or that, or to repent of my sinful ways, or renounce anything. But She gently reproves and encourages. No fire and brimstone! But rather, a softly spoken question or prompting, in the hope that I might take the best course of action.

Karen Webb: That's my experience too, Reg ...and never any judgement. The ache for freedom comes from my response, not anything that's demanded of me. We are allowed to hide under the duvet – and life is so much richer outside. I'm tired and babbling probably repeating myself. Never mind. Hello!

Reg Amor: Hi Karen: Do you find that you are able to 'tune out' as it were? (When sometimes life is overwhelming). But in so doing, it's as though a vital spark of life has been extinguished and life just becomes humdrum and mundane. But on retuning, not even raised eyebrow just a warm embrace! A welcome back and a whispered, 'I'm always here for you'.

Karen Webb: Hi Reg – yes I can and do 'tune out' – and with me it's involuntary and so damned uncomfortable, agonising even, that when I relax and listen I wonder what the hell happened. My way of talking about it is that the automatic psychological defence structure takes over to protect me in times of material difficulty. Like the computer Hal in the film 2001. We all have our Hal – programmed to protect us even when that defence destroys us. For me that's part of what contemplative practice is about – learning how to notice Howell before it takes over.

Reg Amor: Damn that 'Hal'! It's so difficult to find the 'override' button too!

Alix Sandra Huntley-Speirs: I truly believe that a deeply true mystical experience is not possible without a contemplative mind or rather I would say… a Poet's mind. Without that ability to identify the nuances surrounding us, quieting the mind to simply "listen", the experience might just pass us by entirely without our knowledge, shut down to the greater mysteries at play. Maybe for those do not follow this path there are windows into the mystical realms that suddenly emerge in front of them, as if almost by accident. Their own minds slipping naturally into that contemplative mode and allowed access, if only briefly. These experiences can too easily be dismissed by a non-contemplative, by a non-mystic. A true Mystic knows and understands what has occurred and is not only able to work with the information received but also to interact with the energies themselves. It is both a passive and an active exchange of energies, a natural ebb and flow. These events imbue our path and our words, our actions inexorably for the rest of our years, and quite likely beyond …In my mind, there can be no separation of these two concepts.

Ani Ashford: To me the two aspects are steppingstones. One practices contemplation to enter the world of the mystic. However, contemplation does not always end up on the next step up to mysticism. The knowledge progresses bit by bit as I allow myself to 'let go' and let be. It feels like a Fibonacci spiral, or petals on a rose which unfold until the centre is exposed to become the 'Mystic'. In my own contemplation there became these moments where all that was 'me' became conscious of being an infinitesimal, glowing bit in the energy of the Universe. There were no boundaries nor walls, no religion. My energy was joyously dancing with all the other energies. There have been moments of mentally 'seeing' that which was like a movie, perhaps memory bits from my ancestors. I learned from each experience. No, these two concepts cannot truly be separated for they are intertwined as two lovers holding hands.

Appendix 7

Facebook perspectives on pilgrimage

James Nichol How do people feel about pilgrimage as a practice? Any experiences you'd like to share?

Nico Vermaas It is a beautiful way of getting out of the 'comfort zone', which makes it possible for new insights to surface. And the spiritual focus of a pilgrimage opens all kinds of mental gateways, so that these new insights also have spiritual quality. Being an atheist Druid, my pilgrimages take me into the wilderness instead of to religious sites. Or to mythical places. Always to places where physical reality blends with meaningful imagination.

Elaine Knight I've travelled alone or companion/companioning to certain sites a sort of pilgrimage. Malta and Gozo over example. Lake Bala, the Merlin's cave at Tintagel, Caer Laverock in Dumfries and Anglesey to name a few places closer to home. I found Paul Coelho's book *The Pilgrimage*, a bit contrived perhaps but enjoyable.

Bishop Mark Pius Charlton Being in the Maya Homelands I visit the sites quite often. But I do that in two ways. There are visits and there are pilgrimages. For me Pilgrimages are always to sites which I have already been to and connected with the spirits of that place. The pilgrimage from me is to return and reconnect with that energy and those Beings. I never think of a first visit as a pilgrimage as I really go there to see and learn rather than be and connect.

Criss Glover This question has really set me thinking. The first thing I came up with was the Chalice Well in Glastonbury. I'm lucky enough to live about 40 minutes' drive away but even when I lived in Essex it was a place I would return to again and again. Now I live closer I find myself visiting on a monthly basis for spiritual connection and renewal, and, being a Companion, I also go once or twice a year on a largely silent retreat. But I'm not convinced this is a pilgrimage – that word suggests more of a journey than I take, more like the trip I take each year to my parents graves in Yorkshire. It has set me thinking, however, about what would really constitute a pilgrimage for me. Thank you James.

Nico Vermaas Criss, that you were not a Muslim in your previous life.

Elaine Knight For a Muslim the Hajj pilgrimage to Mecca is a major event in life. Wills are written beforehand and they dress in white, leaving the day-to-day behind, even family commitments.

Nico Vermaas The international OBOD camp in the Netherlands?

Criss Glover I visited many sacred sites over the year, my interest in archaeology means I am always finding more, but the most memorable for me where the stones of Carnac in Brittany and the temples of Malta. However I'm selfish and if I'm visiting a site for spiritual purposes I like to have it as far as possible to myself. So I find favourite stone circles like Castlerigg in Cumbria hard to connect with spiritually. Avebury usually does the job though because it's big enough to get away from the crowds and West Kennet Long Barrow in the early morning or evening is a very special place for me.

Nico Vermaas Mmmm most sites I can think of have nothing to do with Druids but are prehistoric sites. Like Stonehenge, New Grange, the Orkneys etc. If you really want to visit ancient Druid sites then you may want to have a look at Mont Beuvraix in Bourgogne (the Celtic town of Bibracte). Or the Celtic graves in Germany (from the time the Celts had not yet reached Britain). But we are not from the Stone Age, nor Celts, I guess we can choose freely. I can't imagine that defining lines were so strict, especially without books or Facebook. Even if they wanted to, I doubt they could communicate a lot of common practices through the different tribes, let alone enforce it. I think it must have be quite organic and diverse. And I guess neo Druidry is that way also.

Pascale Titley When I turned 50 my gift to me was to go to the UK as part of a pilgrimage and experience a sunrise ceremony (with a Tibetan Rinpoche) at Stonehenge, having a 'chance' guided tour by a Druid climbing Mount Silbury then walking to the 'Dragon' Long Barrow (don't remember it's proper name), Avebury, Glastonbury Abbey, the Tor, Tintagel and St. Nectan's Glen in Cornwall. That trip really shook me up in terms of reconnecting with past lives which is why it felt as such a pilgrimage of 'returning'.

Bishop Mark Pius Charlton I have a number of places here in Mexico. I live very close to Palenque. It is a stunning place in the middle of the jungle. It is magical and mystical filled with the energy of Balum (Jaguar). I love Malpasito. That is a Zoque site. I had the privilege of conducting a wedding there. Right at the bottom of the pyramid steps. I truly feel deeply connected there. And the local people made our post-wedding party something to truly remember. Edzna in Campeche is also wonderful. There is a deep sense of peace there. I could go on and on. Let me finish by saying that one of my favourite places to go to when I'm back home in the UK is neither Druid nor Neolithic. But I gain a deep sense of connection when walking on Hadrian's Wall.

Nimue Brown I'd love to walk one but have not had space or time to do so yet. I'd like to walk the old way over the hills to Avebury, it's got a name, but my brain is cheese.

Chris Brolls Each year I do my own little pilgrimage to the Rollright Stones spend around an hour and a half there, I always get there around 6 AM before anyone else then it's off to Wayland's Smithy. Sometimes I will play my drum will play my flute or just meditate. Then it's off to Avebury for more of the same then I finish my travels of Glastonbury Tor.

I always finish the day feeling so good. Charged and full of life.

Pascale Titley Doing the Ridgeway will be something I would love to do ... it will be on my list and I go back to the UK. Is it still available to do nowadays?

Criss Glover Hi Pascale. I would agree going to a special access at Stonehenge where you can get among the stones as opposed to being corralled along designated path can be magical. If the Long Barrow you visited is at Avebury I guess it will be West Kennett, which is one of my favourite places, but keep quiet climbing Silbury Hill LOL. Since a hole appeared in the top and needed some reconstruction work climbing it is forbidden (although I did myself leg over the barbed wire with my young daughter to climb it many years ago and remember climbing it as a child on holiday). The Ridgeway is one of the oldest tracks in the country. It really connects you to the ancestors walking the track has been walked since prehistoric times, mind you it's 87 miles long. I've done bits of it but would need serious training to tackle it all!! I had forgotten about St. Nectan's Glen IMO the most beautiful waterfall in the world and a truly magical place.

Pascal Titley Criss Glover... yes the Long Barrow was at Avebury we could see it from the top of Silbury Hill and yes we climbed over the barbed wire!!! But at that point my attitude was that I am turning 50 ... the worst that will happen they will put me in jail and I was hoping that an English jail would be quite civilised and might even serve tea!!! <Grin>. And at St. Nectan's Glen, I took pictures with dozens of orbs being part of it ... it was quite amazing. The one place I didn't mention was also when you are sitting on top of the cliff (by a small church) at sunset, and you look across the sea at Tintagel and the Dragon is there in plain sight, immortalised in the cliff but there nonetheless ...

Thomas Harris In 2000 I had the experience of going to where my Ancestors were from in the Cherokee homelands outside Atlanta, Georgia. It gave me a perspective on familial kinship I will never be able to replace.

JJ Middleway Apart from places already mentioned I would say that Iona is a wonderful Druid pilgrimage. Just getting there is a pilgrimage in itself; from south-west England it's a train journey up to Glasgow than a beautiful ride up the West Coast of Scotland. A ferry over the waters from Oban to Mull, a bus journey across Mull and a ferry to Iona itself and a true sense of arriving somewhere sacred. The old Gaelic name for the island was the Isle of Druids and is not for nothing that Kings from four countries, including many Kings of Scotland (including Macbeth) are buried there. I have been several times and never fails to inspire and infuse me with awe and Awen. The best bet for accommodation these days is the new youth hostel at the north of the island. Clean and friendly. Camping is generally not allowed on the island but I used to benefit from the generosity of a lovely lady called Mrs. Macfadyen who was Druid friendly. I'll never forget the haunting sound of corncrakes flying overhead, in the evening dusk in the wilds where she allowed three pilgrim Druids to camp.

Karen Webb It's striking, as someone who just joined the thread, that although the journey not the destination has been mentioned, mostly (not all, apologies to you) this is about important places to visit. People speak about pilgrimage to their local sacred sites, or "I try to visit". Surely, pilgrimage is about the journey not the destination? And for me, anything that involves less than many days walk is not really a pilgrimage. Except of course for those who cannot walk for whatever reason (that includes me) – and that just means many days travel instead. I know this sounds and is positional, and I need to revisit the word. Still, I know many pagans who have done the Santiago Compostella route and loved it despite, or including, the Christian emphasis. Records indicate it was a pre-Christian route, but that's not the point. For me pilgrimage means casting off, taking to the road, becoming face-to-face with yourself, for long enough to learn something from the journey not the destination. Visiting sacred sites is necessary and powerful and not the definition of pilgrimage.

James Nichol Thanks Karen for making the distinction between visiting sacred sites and pilgrimage it helps me with both.

Karen Webb Thanks James – your video too speaks of the casting off. Seems to me that that's integral to pilgrimage? And can't be done in a day. That's in no way to deny or belittle the journey to visit one of the sacred sites, and be blessed by it and the journey. Is there a word for the pilgrimage that happens in the space of one day? Surely there is, somewhere in Old English or Gaelic, as it must be, and probably was once, honoured.

JJ Middleway Well said Karen, regarding pilgrimage as the journey. The most Druidic pilgrimage I've ever experienced was in 1997 when I visited what I reckoned to be the seven most ancient trees on this island. All yew trees, as you might have guessed. I didn't walk all round England Scotland and Wales but I did do an awful lot of walking and a lot of searching guided by double rainbows believe it or not. There was a real sense of journeying which culminated at my favourite tree in Wales where spent I three days and nights (72 hours) inside the tree (it was hollow) without food or water. A total fusion of contemplation and mysticism now I come to think of it. It worked wonderfully well for me in that time. However I'm not recommending it of itself, but more as an example.

I would say from personal experience that the Ridgeway is a great Pilgrimage route with the wonders of the Uffington White Horse, Dragon Hill, Wayland's Smithy (an ancient burial mound) and dramatic arrival at Avebury. Finally, one of the fascinating things about my relationship to Iona in terms of pilgrimage is that they were going to build a bridge over to the island from Mull (to 'make it easier') and that would have killed it for me. Luckily they thought better of it. The sense of making a significant effort to get somewhere; of its 'otherness'; its separation from normality; all these make for aspects of pilgrimage in my experience.

Karen Webb Thank you JJ for these words: "The sense of making a significant effort to get somewhere; of its 'otherness' and separation from normality all these micro-aspects of the pilgrimage in my experience". Yes and for your tale ...The Story of the Yews should be one of our Bardic staples. Would you craft it for us?

JJ Middleway Goodness me, now there's something. Maybe it's something we each craft for ourselves. I'll give it some thought; but where would I put it (dear Lisa, dear Lisa)? ... There's a hole in your yew tree, dear Henry dear Henry.

Karen Webb Sudden thought – looking at how many people think of going to a sacred place as pilgrimage: is it also about going home?

JJ Middleway Absolutely

Karen Webb JJ you could always put it on the Bardic pages of the Druid Network website – dear Henry! Or send me your rough draft I'll be your Lisa. Do you know I'll now be hearing that in my head till after I sleep? Tells our age!

JJ Middleway Bless you and thank you! Tis time I wrote it up properly. Rather a busy summer but later in the autumn is possible. We'll see.

Karen Webb Fruits to be gathered, laid by. In the right season. Maybe we might share your fruits around a fire one day, maybe not. Let me know though, when the harvest has happened?

Dawn N Jodie Diaz-Ruiz As an American, this question got me wondering about pilgrimage routes on this side of the Pond. Do any and if you have ideas were experience with this? I'm not Native American, and my family only goes back about three generations in this country. I don't have the ancestral ties here that Thomas spoke of. Or is it that the journey is the goal of that something like hiking the Appalachian Trail (which runs from Maine to Georgia) would make a pilgrimage, rather than going to visit a specific site (maybe the Grand Canyon, for example).

JJ Middleway Hi Dawn. I would say that although relationships with the land forged over time by our ancestors make for a rich and in-depth pilgrimage experience, it is for each of us to forge our own relationship with the land. I don't think you're especially disadvantaged. I'm pure English with not a drop of English blood in me in either line: when it comes to pilgrimage may be the year that even helps – (natural wanderer). I think the trick is to tune into the land wherever you find yourself and feel what might want to take you. What is calling? What gives meaning and purpose to your journey – the journey of your soul? Usually the soul knows only too well where pilgrimage needs to go. It is just a case of making time and quality space available for it to have a chance to come through – hence contemplation! And then having the courage literally 'the rage of the heart' to follow it through. Anyhow my own experience is that life itself is the true pilgrimage (if I dare open up to it) and that the mini pilgrimage are wonderful reminders and refreshes of that.

Dawn N Jodie Diaz Ruiz Thank you for your wisdom JJ. I like your life-as-pilgrimage idea a lot. I've long seen life as a journey so your idea of life as the pilgrimage with mini-pilgrimages is very helpful. I think I need to think on this more.

JJ Middleway And yes. Something like the Appalachian Trail (which I dreamed of doing when I read about it in the National Geographical Magazine many years ago) would fit the bill of pilgrimage – a journey, rather than the Grand Canyon (a destination).There is something more than merely walking trail however. It is to do with 'the Intent' we bring to it. Somehow making it sacred, rather than merely functional. That's what makes the Via de Compostella so special. Countless thousands have walked that route in an attitude of reverent mirth; it cannot help but infuse those who follow. No matter whether Christian, Agnostic or Druid. So either plug into one of the old paths of your land or start your own. Approached in Reverence (with a smile) is how all pilgrimages are started. Someone has to be first ...

Appendix 8

The contributors

David Popely

David Popely is a Druid and Devotional Polytheist. A Londoner by birth, he now lives in rural Somerset. He is a husband, sole practitioner accountant, chess-player, cricket scorer, guitarist, burgeoning mandolin-player and quartermaster to two daft, lazy cats.

Elaine Knight

I have been a librarian, psychotherapist, human potential facilitator and the High Priestess of a Wiccan Coven. I have designed and facilitated Pagan Federation open rituals, been a Pagan Celebrant and a *Pagan Dawn* book reviews editor. Now retired, I still dance the Spiral with those I love but at a slower pace. I celebrate being an artist, poet and contemplative Druid.

www.elaineknight.tumblr.com

www.art4nowelaineknight.carbonmade.com

Eve Adams

Eve Adams lives in the woods and fields on the edge of the Cotswold escarpment. She has a large wildlife garden. In the darker seasons she makes needle felted and embroidered pictures inspired by the Mantle of the Goddess. Otherwise she is a psychotherapist and supervisor of longstanding. Her healing and spiritual pursuits find a home and belonging in Druidry.

www.soultides.org.uk

James Nichol

I am an OBOD Druid and mentor. This book draws on my work and development in both roles. It also owes something to earlier involvements with humanistic and transpersonal counselling and psychology, and to a doctoral project on creative ageing that included an exploration of spirituality in the second half of life (*Social spaces for mature imaginations: reflections on a participative inquiry*. University of the West of England, 2007).

http://contemplativeinquiry.wordpress.com

JJ Middleway

JJ is fully living his Druidry in the world by offering rituals and celebrations, singing and healing, in reverence and mirth; for people, places and planet, through the medicine of Love (with a smile).

Joanna Vander Hoeven

Joanna Vander Hoeven has written two books: *Zen Druidry: Living a Natural Life With Full Awareness* and *Dancing With Nemetona: A Druid's Exploration of Sanctuary and Sacred Space*. Her third book, *The Awen Alone: Walking the Path of*

The Solitary Druid is due for release late 2014. She is a regular blogger for Moon Books, SageWoman.

www.downtheforestpath.wordpress.com.

www.joannavanderhoeven.com.

Karen Webb

Karen is a passionate, lifelong student and teacher of spirituality, comparative religion and psychology and lives in Malvern, UK.

Julie Bond

Julie came to Druidry through the OBOD correspondence course which she began in 1992. In 1994 she began to develop her Druid practice in a contemplative/monastic way and in 2010 she joined the Order of the Sacred Nemeton (OSN), a contemplative Druid monastic order. She comes originally from Liverpool and grew up in Formby, on the North West coast of England. She now lives in London.

Katy Jordan

I'm a country-woman born and bred, growing up in the Vale of Pewsey, poised between Avebury and Stonehenge. I live in West Wiltshire and work at the University of Bath. I'm a librarian, an author, a folklorist, a family historian, and a Druid contemplative. I love to get out into nature, walking the land, paddling the waterways. I do far too much of everyday trivia, and don't do enough of the things that really matter. I aspire to change this.

Mark Rosher

Mark is a practising self-identified Druid living in the West of England. A professional engineer about to leave it all for a new life, he is also a charity trustee of the Druid Network and Chairman of his local Parish Council. Husband, father, brother, son, and a lover of the outdoors, occasionally on a motorcycle.

Nimue Brown

Nimue Brown has written assorted books on Druid and Pagan subjects and blogs regularly. OBOD trained, and also a volunteer there, she nonetheless tends towards more feral and improvised approaches to Druidry. Her work life in Green politics and as a professional blogger has her running about like a mad thing, and the respite of contemplation keeps her passably sane.

www.druidlife.wordpress.com.

Penny Billington

Penny Billington (Somerset) is an active member in the Order of Bards, Ovates, and Druids and she edits the Order magazine *Touchstone*. She regularly runs workshops, organizes rituals, and gives lectures. She is also the author of *The Path of Druidry: Walking the Ancient Green Way* and two druidic mystery novels.

www.pennybillington.co.uk

Robert Kyle

Robert Kyle is an artist, writer and member of OBOD; he has studied teachings for many years from indigenous cultures such as Yungdrung Bon and Peruvian Shamanism, both have enriched his understanding of spirituality in the west. He is currently working on a project looking at the concepts of enlightenment in Druidry.

Rosa Davis

I am an artist and retired trainer of counsellors. I began sitting in meditation 40 years ago and have explored many different traditions over the years. Since 2000 my practice has been held within a Druid Sacred Circle. I am a mentor for the OBOD correspondence course, and I live in Stroud with my third husband.

Tom Brown

Druid and illustrator, walker, dreamer, lunatic.

Made in the USA
Lexington, KY
15 November 2014